The Urban Connection Project was established for the purpose of raising the odds of success for systematically disadvantaged students in urban schools. Our education consultants are passionate about raising up our next generation of leaders to be accountable, trust-worthy, critically thinking individuals who can keep our nation globally competitive. We believe that some of the greatest minds are waiting to be recognized and nurtured to maximum potential through several avenues, both inside and outside of the classroom. Educators have the single-most direct impact on the youth and therefore systems of structure must be present in management and instruction in order to meet students where they are and assist them to a level of mastery and excellence.

The Urban Connection Project's approach to service delivery is unique in the fact that we truly despise a "one size fits all" approach to educational reform. We recognize that we are not the only sources of expertise and we consider ourselves facilitating agents of change in the process to increased advocacy and achievement for the students affected by our work. Although we have successful experiences implementing systems and research-based practices, we would be doing a disservice to our clients and ourselves if we did not take the time to customize our services to each school's needs. Because of this, The Urban Connection Project strongly discourages the adoption of our practices without allowing us to first conduct observations and collect on-site research.

For questions, comments or to partner with The Urban Connection Project, please contact us:

Admin@TheUrbanConnectionProject.org

or visit us online:

TheUrbanConnectionProject.org

Dedication

This book is dedicated to my mother, Willa Mae Stallings-Canty and my grandmother, Gladys Jean Stallings. They started and ran a very successful summer program in Detroit, MI called IALAC (I Am Loveable And Capable) for 30+ years. It is because of their love, adoration and sacrifice to impact the lives of tens of thousands of youth that my passion began. Their legacy lives on through me and I thank God for the example they provided on how to live in your purpose and impact communities through education.

To My Wife

Thank you for supporting my dreams, chasing yours, and impacting the lives of youth through education and mentoring. I couldn't imagine a better partner to be on this journey with than you.

Act 1

Finding My Place as an Educator

Intro

I couldn't believe it. Another passionate and courageous teacher who made the amiable and brave decision to teach our inner-city students, gone. I couldn't say I was surprised, but I didn't expect it that early. It's ironic how prepared people are when they decide to move to a different country, but neglect that same preparation when they go to teach in an area much different from the one they experienced as a child. Our country is huge and there is no program at any college or university that can prepare you for every classroom, school, school district or student you will service. Our university's job is to prepare us to educate. It is OUR job to evolve the training we receive to fit the school demographics we ultimately want to reach. I think it's crazy how the importance of this transition is overlooked.

But that's neither here nor there. What was I going to do? What were we going to do? Other teaching candidates were denied because the school believed in him and now look what happened. It was hard enough for our principal to find a teacher in the summer; it would be even harder to find a replacement since school had started. It was so selfish of me to only think from the adult's perspective. What about the students? We were supposed to coach them to be prepared for the world. Some of them were fighting to keep their head above water in school while they struggled with a parent or guardian who walked out of their life. Now, a teacher left, proving their perception on what reality is. A teacher was given the opportunity to change their perspective for the better but only ended up confirming.

Even worse, the students would be stuck in a chain of substitute teachers without a curriculum to follow. They may as well just be a glorified "babysitter:" someone certified to be in the classroom with the students (since we have to have someone in there by law). But, what about the students!? They were going to miss so much instruction and wherever they end up next year will have required prerequisites for certain classes. Goodbye, honors classes. Goodbye, AP classes junior/senior year. Goodbye, feeling like you belong and can compete academically with anyone.

He left our school and didn't think twice about it. I wondered if it will haunt him. I wondered if abandonment will have a domino effect to students dropping out. Often, a student falls behind and has trouble catching back up so they say, 'forget it.' A year without instruction could lead to educational destruction.

As you read my story, understand that you can be a successful teacher in an urban, or low-income area. You can be confident no matter your background. Your effectiveness is not determined by your skin tone or gender. You will be successful because you put in the work to prepare yourself for the specific school you will be working at. The strategies you put into place will work wonders in your classroom. But, you must be willing to adapt.

What about me? How did I begin teaching? Why was I successful? Why did I decide to work with underprivileged students? Simply put, I focused on the bigger picture. A teacher needs to adapt to the students just as much as the students to the teacher. I was willing to be what I needed to be for the students to succeed.

Lesson 1

The Presence of Hope
January 17ᵗʰ, 2012 it began

I graduated college 4 weeks prior to that day with a degree in Secondary Education Mathematics with a minor in Communications. I completed the rigorous coursework and department requirements to prove myself worthy of handling the noble task of producing America's future leaders. Excitement, slight nervousness and joy filled my body for what the next step would encompass.

Until this point, I was a semi-adult. I had the responsibility of being on my own, but my parents were there for me if I fell short financially. Although a parent's love will never fade, there is an unspoken mutual agreement shared between parent and offspring at age 18 or after college: "I have done my job, now it's your turn." I was ready. Having a degree in mathematics gave me many options across the country to consider for work but I actually didn't have to choose the location to begin my journey.

There was a beautiful young lady, whom I had grown very fond of, that decided to move to Phoenix, Arizona to become an educator. True and genuine love is extremely rare and hard to find, so it was easy to make the decision to relocate. That way, I could chase my future wife and prepare our nation's next generation to succeed in life at the same time. Little did I know, Phoenix was going to be completely different than anything I had experienced.

As the youngest of 3 boys, I grew up in Detroit, Michigan. Growing up in a tough city (with bullying brothers) helped develop my fearless mentality. This trait helped me tremendously with facing new challenges in my new career, so Phoenix would be a task I was willing to accept. During my 3rd grade year, we relocated to the suburbs. Both neighborhoods had a lot of children, but the way we played put many things in perspective.

Playing outside with my friends in Detroit, the only instruction we heard from parents was "make sure you are back in time for dinner." Or, "be home before the street lights come on." We played games like Hide-and-Seek, "Pick 'Em Up, Mess 'Em Up" (a variation of football in which there is no clear goal other than tackle the person with the ball. I honestly don't think there was a way to win). We also played basketball whenever we could.

Living in Lathrup Village (the suburb), we never played Pick 'Em Up, Mess 'Em Up. We played Hide-and-Seek but it definitely wasn't as aggressive, and no one really argued or complained about cheating. We played basketball too, but also street hockey and street soccer. The parents were much more hands on with making sure they knew exactly where the kids were. They taught their children foundational ideals to success by encouraging how to set up a lemonade stand, strategically sell Girl Scout cookies, etc. I thoroughly enjoyed growing up in both neighborhoods, however, inner-city living allowed me see and understand the differences. This is what lit a fire in me to motivate the under-privileged students I would eventually work with.

During the summers, I was consumed by a summer camp called I.A.L.A.C. (I Am Loveable And Capable) founded by my mother and grandmother. This camp was in the heart of the city and serviced kids in Detroit and metro Detroit. Kids from ages 4-16 were welcome to attend (including me). IALAC was a Monday-Thursday day camp. Monday and Tuesday, the youth moved from class to class for the day where qualified instructors offered classes such as Cooking, Theatre, Music, Peace Center (handling situations without violence), Physical Education, Reading and Teen Center.

On Wednesday we would attend a computer class at Wayne State University and walk around campus to help get the youth in the mindset of the possibility of a college education. Thursday was usually a fun day trip to a waterpark, the science center, a carnival, etc. There were years my mother and grandmother got paid for their services from grants and enrollment. But, there were also darker years where funds were not available. No matter the circumstance, they worked tirelessly to ensure it was an amazing summer for each camper to remember.

I can recall years where they decided not to pay themselves at all to make sure there were enough funds for the counselors, many of whom had been former campers. Sometimes, they would cut the cost in half, or bypass the registration fee completely to service as many youth as possible. Although it was a huge sacrifice, it was one of the first examples of true passion I ever witnessed.

I attended as a camper for 9 years before I became a counselor at age 13. I'd like to say it was because I was so great and prepared, but I think having a prenatal connection with the camp director helped get me the job. Either way, I began working with kids. After being a camp counselor for 9 years, I decided I wanted more. I wanted to lead the camp. I gained so much experience and learned so much in school about working with youth that I was ready to be the camp director. My mother and Grandmother ran the camp for 30 years and were excited to see me grow into a leader. We decided an Assistant Director position would be the best start. I suggested co-assistant directorship and told them about this young lady I knew named Kristen, who also had a strong passion and desire for youth. I also expressed how organized and task oriented she was and explained how we could run the program together.

They agreed and decided to bring us both in to discuss our roles. Before our first meeting, I received a phone call from my grandmother. Usually if she called around this time of the year it was to talk or create a game-plan about the summer program. This time it was a little different.

"Why are you so passionate about bringing this young lady in to help? Is this a girl you are dating?"

I assured her that we were just friends (which we were at the time) and to give her a chance. I guess I forgot that my Grandmother had been around the block a few times and knew how love began. Whether she continued to have thoughts or not, she respected my request and left it alone.

After the first meeting, our roles were set and we were ready to plan and prepare. I was in charge of organizing the field trips and dealing with behavior issues. I was tasked with developing a system specifically for our camp that was fair, understood by all, and progressive. Part of my job was also to involve the parents any way possible. Our first summer was phenomenal and the kids raved about how much fun it was. The system for discipline, getting parents involved, being direct and consistent, and connecting with the youth on a personal level, really allowed our program to flourish.

I returned for 2 additional years to direct the camp, which helped me in preparation to teach. Attending college equipped me to teach content but directing the summer program helped me realize how important relationship building, trust, fairness and structure are. Many students in lower-income societies come from households where those fundamentals may not be present. This is not always because of a lack in effort on the parent's (or guardian's) behalf. It is very possible the student lives in a single-parent household where the mother/father is working many jobs in order to provide. The student may be one of many siblings where they don't get the attention they need. Or, the student may have had issues like those that I dealt with.

My scholastic career was one heck of a roller coaster. From early elementary to 5th grade, I had never received a "C" on my report card. Between 6th grade and 10th grade, I did the bare minimum to pass and from 11th grade to 12th grade, I was on the "High Honor Roll." Simply looking at my grades, one could assume that I became irresponsible or that my parents became lax. One could even assume that I was finding myself, but it was much deeper than that. Divorce.

My parents went through a gruesome, seemingly endless divorce and it took a toll on me. My mother never let me fall behind as I was growing up but once the divorce process began, her life shifted completely. My mother was a stay-at-home mom who supported my father as he was the bread-winner of the family. Once the thought of no longer having that income emerged, my mother decided to get a job and go back to school full-time to attain her bachelor's degree. As she divided the time she used to give to us between a job and school, I was able to fall between the cracks. Was she concerned? Of course. Did I get punished? Absolutely, but it was hard to find comfort knowing my father would not be living with us anymore and my mother's 1-2 hours of attention a day did not suffice. For about 5 scholastic years I saw more of my teachers than I did my parents (do the simple math: 7-8 hours at school). I liked going to school because it was a break from reality. However, I never did my homework, I argued with authority and I did the bare minimum so that I wouldn't have to face repeating a grade level. I was looking for comfort. I was looking for something to show me that what I was going through was not standard and I didn't find that something until 11th grade.

What I found comfort in was hope: the hope of a brighter tomorrow, a more bountiful life and the idea that I could get to college. Once a student thinks they have nothing to hope for, they stop trying. That can manifest in a student having such a low grade that they know they can't get it up to pass the class. It can also manifest in a student not thinking they can make it in life and be successful. When they become hopeless, they stop caring. ***Our students need to feel the presence of hope.*** Just think about it. Imagine a student has a 22% grade in your class and you have a policy in place where you do not accept late work. That student knows that no matter how well they do on the final 3 tests and how much homework they turn in henceforth, they will still get an "F." Why would they try? Imagine your school district does not retain students to repeat a grade and you have a student in your 6th grade class with a 1st grade reading ability. Yet, you continue not to scaffold and modify the work to meet them where they are ability-wise. Why would they try? It is not just our duty to teach, it's our duty to create hope and inspire. Students need to feel there is something attainable to work towards. If they lack that presence of hope, then issues emerge concerning behavior (often rebellion) and attendance.

I felt hope for the first time, in a long time, in 11th grade when a speaker stood on stage at my school and asked what our next step was. He asked us not to get caught up in today and to focus on tomorrow. He urged us to think about where we wanted our life to be in 5 years and talked to us about how we write our own destiny. If we get there, it would be because of us. If we don't, there would be no one else to blame.

I can remember thinking about the successful role models in my life. The extremely successful technology business my mother's family owned (Sync Technologies) and how nothing was handed to them. They had to work hard to get every penny they earned. I recalled thinking about how much time I had left to do better when I was in middle school, but that time slowly diminished. In that moment, that message was all I needed to hear. He introduced hope back into my life and I was ready to try again.

As a teacher, I knew I would face students going through similar, and even worse, situations and I wanted to make sure I was prepared to be an effective and contributing member of the village it takes to raise the child. After my graduation from college. I took a couple of weeks to gather myself before I went to Phoenix, ready and eager to make a difference. January 17th, 2012. My journey began.

Self-Reflection

1) Sometimes, we need to remind ourselves why we began the journey we are on. There will be sunny days, happy moments and joyous occasions that ensue and it's easy to continue during those times but what about roadblocks, rocky roads and bad weather? They can derail our thoughts and make us rethink why we ever began. Low moments should never trump your purpose. They are guaranteed to happen but do not present themselves to make you quit or give up: they are opportunities for growth. While you're growing from those moments, think back to the beginning of why you're here and what you hope to accomplish and allow those thoughts to fuel you to continue.

Why did you begin teaching?

Why did you choose to teach in the area you are in?

2) An absence of hope can ruin an entire community. When you have nothing to hope for or when you lose hope, your entire mood and outlook changes. For most of us who played sports growing up, making it to the big league was a dream and something we hoped would happen. Somewhere along the road we realized it was a long shot and even further down that path we realized it wouldn't happen. Think about the shift you made when you realized making it to the professional level was not attainable. You began to think about Plan

B, gave less time and effort in your sport and your mind refocused somewhere else. Our students can experience the same thing and it's our job to convince them otherwise. What can you do to ignite that hope? Maybe you know someone from their neighborhood who is now successful that can come and speak. Hang pictures in your room of inspirational figures or quotes. Create an individualized plan with that student who is failing your class that outlines how the student can pull their grade up and pass. Whatever the case may be, keep your standards high and the student's hope alive. Students do not need expectations lowered. They need us to coach them into believing their dreams can be reached.

What strategies can you utilize to introduce/inspire/reignite hope in a student?

Lesson 2

Draw Upon Your Own Experiences
The Job Hunt

I landed in Phoenix, Arizona in the evening and was met by this beautiful young lady who was full of charm and charisma. I knew upon arriving that I wanted to take our relationship as far as it could go but I had little understanding of the exact path to get there. All I knew was the obvious: It's hard to grow together when there's 2,500 miles between you (duh). The purpose of my trip to Phoenix was to 1) grow closer to my girlfriend and 2) find a job. My priorities were definitely in that order. I had just graduated from college! Including Kindergarten, I had spent the last 17 years learning and earned some well needed time off.

Having a girlfriend who is full of energy, spunk and drive also comes with questions of "Well, what are you doing while I'm at work?" or "When are you going to look for a job?" These were expected and that was part of the reason I was attracted to her. I looked at her then, and I still look at her now, thinking 'I can't wait for my daughter to be just like you.' Though it is a sweet thought, it did not answer her question.

"I am going to look for a job soon, babe. I promise. I was thinking about starting my search next week." Being understanding of what it felt like to finally be out of college, the answer sufficed and we continued our conversation about a different topic. I was willing to conquer the world, but was not quite ready. I needed some sleep, rest and relaxation for a week, or two, before I wanted to begin, or so I thought.

Kristen was raised in a family that was full of "go-getters" and drive. She was born the youngest of three in the city my college was located: Kalamazoo, Michigan. Her mother was an educator and preached the same principles to her children that educators teach students. Going to college, being involved in programs outside of school and having a job, once you were of age, were not options, they were expectations. At a young age, she chose to learn how to ice-skate (a parent's dream, financially) and after years and years of early-morning practices, training sessions and competitions, she ended up trying out for the local university while she was in high school. Lo' and behold, she made the team. This team ended up being amongst the best teams in the country and represented our

United States of America in many competitions against other nations in her last two years of high school.

If she wanted to move forward with her skating career, she had great potential and the opportunity to do so. Why didn't she, you ask? Well, she also played basketball growing up. Her older brother was a legend in their high school (and still holds a few records). He was extremely passionate about basketball and Kristen didn't fall too far from that tree. Along with skating, she also made her varsity basketball team by her sophomore year. She practiced daily and worked to become the best she could be at the sport. Her love for basketball led her to many club basketball tournaments and time spent in the gym to get better. She told me stories of her typical high school day and how she would wake up early to be at skate practice at 5:30AM, then would leave for school (and was dual enrolled at Western Michigan University). After school, she had basketball practice for her high school team and afterwards, since she was of age to work, she would leave practice and squeeze in an hour or two at her job. Most amazingly, she STILL finished High School with a 3.7 GPA (I know. I got tired just writing about how long her days were).

She could have spent time pursuing a career in sports, as she had many options, but her passion ended up taking a turn. Her mother was the head of a vacation bible school for a week every summer for children ages

5-16 in the city of Kalamazoo, MI. Some of the youth, who attended this camp, were from families with strong parental figures and great home lives. But others were from households in which food wasn't guaranteed. They lived in neighborhoods where gang violence or drug related activities were very possible. Many of them lived in single-parent households. Kristen went to this camp as a kid and saw the others as friends. However, at a young age she realized they all lived the same life at camp, but their lives at home were much different.

Once she became of age, her mother brought her on staff to help create activities, facilitate operations and counsel. Between that experience and growing up with her mother being an educator, her love, compassion and drive to improve the lives of underprivileged students emerged. As much as you try to deny a passion, you can't run from what you were called to do. Kristen spent the first semester of college pursuing a pre-med degree, but after reassessing where her heart was she made the noble decision to be an educator. The program she chose at Michigan State University: The Urban Cohort of Elementary Education. Her strides to improve the lives of students in at-risk communities led me to ask her to help direct the IALAC Summer Program, which she did for two years.

Eventually Kristen's passion led her to intern in Detroit, MI and coach several of her school's basketball teams.

She impressed everyone in her internship and decided to accept the full-time position she was offered at that school. What she didn't know was that Detroit's education system would take a huge turn. Detroit was in disarray and the government appointed an emergency manager to try to help the city get back on its feet. This emergency manager decided to clean up our schools and get rid of any teacher who was not certified (which ended up being many teachers). Although this may have been a good start to fixing the issues facing schools in Detroit, it came with a side-effect: there was a freeze placed on hiring new teachers.

Kristen finished her internship, graduated from college and had a summer to hope for the freeze to be lifted. She was hired by the school and given keys to her room, but without the paperwork going through she would have to work for free. There's no telling how long this would last but she was patient. August came and there was still no lifting of the freeze, so Kristen did what any other college graduate looking for a steady paying job would do: she applied for other jobs. After weeks of applying, she ended up getting a phone call from a school district in Phoenix, Arizona about a 3rd grade position they needed filled. After a quick phone interview, they set up a time for the second meeting: a video conference call. This video conference call was immediately followed by an offer, which she accepted.

Excited, prepared and ready, she was off to the other side of the America to teach in, what had once been, the lowest income district in the nation. Although it was hard leaving the Detroit school where her heart was, she knew there were students all over who needed what she could offer. Since she started teaching in Phoenix two months after school began, she knew she had work to do. I'll spare you the unnecessary, dramatic set-up many authors try to make and let you know that your thoughts are right: if she could handle skating for Team USA, playing varsity basketball, receiving a 3.7 GPA (while being dual-enrolled in college) and making time for a side job, then she could handle this task as well.

She had a very successful first few months and her administration quickly learned that she could handle any student, no matter how unruly, disobedient or unenthusiastic they were. She had very strict rules with a fun rewards program. She had high expectations for her students both academically and behavior-wise. She built relationships with each of her students and made sure to communicate with the parents about how their child was performing in class. The school raved about her (and even switched some students who needed that type of instruction from their home-class to hers). The state testing benchmark results also reinforced that this Phoenix school had landed a star in the interview process. It was the 4th month of her first year and the only thing she had not quite prepared for was her boyfriend deciding to move to Phoenix with her.

"I am going to look for a job soon, babe. I promise. I was thinking about starting my search next week," I said. Although she was very understanding, she still decided to take on my job hunt by making suggestions. I can remember it like it was yesterday. We arrived at her apartment and I unloaded my things. She was so excited that I was there but still needed to prepare herself for bed. It was a Monday and she was teaching the next day. I understood and stayed quiet long enough for her to get to sleep then I also closed my eyes.

The next day, she kissed me goodbye as she went off to school. I took that day to get my thoughts together about my next move. I was ready to get started in this next chapter of life (It's always funny to make book references in a book) but first, rest. Kristen came home and asked what I did all day. I responded. She was ok with me taking the day off but asked if I wanted to come to school with her the next day. "I told the kids about you and have pictures of you in the class, so they are excited to finally meet you."

"Of course I will," I said. I'm not a big 'get your rest' kind of guy either. I come from a household where I was never allowed to just sit. We had to be active and were also expected to go to college. My mother raised me to be driven, passionate and whatever word is the opposite of lazy. After my one day, I was ready to see Phoenix. We woke up the next day and went to the school. I spent the day watching what her agenda was like and seeing how involved and excited the students were. I was impressed. "Pretty good for a Michigan State grad," I jokingly said. I'm a University of Michigan fan first and I like rubbing it in her face.

"But you didn't even go there. You went to Western Michigan. We call fans who didn't attend the school 'Walmart Fans' since that's probably where you buy your school gear from. Besides, Michigan State has the best elementary education program in the country." I looked it up, and it was true (that doesn't stop me from poking fun though).

Part of the conversation on our way home was "Do you think you would want to go to my district office to ask about openings?" She worked in a K-8 district. My entire collegiate career I envisioned working with older students. I even did my internship at a local Kalamazoo high school. The reason I liked high school was because the students were one-step away from being adults. I felt like I had the chance to reach them before they were expected to be contributing members of society.

It's crazy some of the things I saw while interning. There were fights, drugs, gang violence, and even students confronting teachers (not often, but there were a few instances). You could see notes being passed and think "oh they're just flirting," but then find out they were passing drugs. I remember during lunch one day, a security guard was in our room and someone contacted him on his walkie-talkie saying 'fight in cafeteria B. I repeat, fight in cafeteria B.' He was in no hurry to go and break it up. Seeing him calm made me ask him why he seemed so relaxed, and this is what he said as he walked off:

"If I break up a fight in the beginning, the kids will still have so much energy left. Also, they didn't get their point across. If they don't settle it now in a safe environment, they may try to settle it outside of school with weapons or no supervision."

Even though his methods were different (I am in no way supporting this, or suggesting it as something you should try), I could understand his logic. He'd rather them fight in a building where they had to walk through a metal-detector to get in, than to take to the streets.

Schools in higher socio-economic societies have issues, but they don't settle them with violence nearly as often. I knew there was a deep insecurity that needed to be addressed. You would be surprised at the types of actions that take place where hope no longer exists.

Hope. Keep that in mind. It's exactly what helped me change my life around and it's the most important thing to inspire in a student. They must have something to hope for. I can remember my mother telling me at an early age to 'never fight someone without something to lose.' That can easily translate to 'never fight someone with an absence of hope.' Part of our jobs as teachers is to provide something for them to hope for: college is typically the most used. My reasons for working with high school students was to reach them before they aren't given a second chance.

"Do you think you would want to go to my district office to ask about open teacher positions?" Kristen hinted at again. She kept bringing up how I needed to apply for a teaching position and I knew those hints would continue until I actually did it. I figured I could try working in a middle school. I've never met a challenge I was afraid of accepting. I didn't see any harm in just visiting the office to inquire.

Originally, I planned on applying for jobs the next week, but time never forgives us for wasting it (something I learned in college). I knew I needed to make the most of my opportunities. After walking into the office with my resume and portfolio, I asked the receptionist about job openings. She indicated that there were many and summoned the hiring manager for the district. After John came to the front, he asked what school I went to and what my major was. I let him know my degree was in Secondary Education Mathematics and his eyes lit up. His immediate response was "we DEFINITELY have job openings for middle school math: 3, to be exact. Give me your information and resumé and we will set up a time for you to speak with one of our principals."

We set up an interview for Friday. At Friday's interview, after a 20-minute conversation with the principal, I was hired. I was asked to start on January 31st and was given a packet of papers to fill out. Kristen and I were so excited for me to get my first paying job. I knew I had to pull everything I learned together to knock this opportunity out of the park. This was not only an opportunity to impress my administration, it was also the chance to enter students' lives to make a difference. I began to prepare, as I knew I was also turning the page to start a new paragraph in my life (I just crack myself up).

Self-Reflection

We all have struggled at some point and if you plan on working with underprivileged youth, you can draw upon those struggles to help bridge the gap between you and them? This connection should not be forced or faked. If your struggle is that your family lost $300k in real estate during the recession, that does not quite relate to a student who has bounced around from foster care to foster care. Honestly, your struggle does not always have to be deep. Maybe you didn't make the basketball team when you tried out. Maybe the girl you liked ended up dumping you. It's possible you had a hard time fitting in at school when you were their age. You may even have grown up in a single-parent household. Whatever the case may be, you can use it to help connect (when applicable). Before our students know who we are, they see us for our outward appearance and in many cases, our outward appearance does not inspire. It's the connection that allows the student to feel that they, too, can be successful.

What hard times have you had to deal with in your life and how did you overcome those obstacles?

Lesson 3

Research Your Clientele
The First Day of School

Walking into the classroom to begin teaching on the first day of school can be difficult enough but starting in the middle of the year is a different story. I knew I was entering a situation where my preparation would be crucial, and I needed to be as versed in what to expect as possible. So, I began my "research."

I began to gather as much information as I could by first calling Principal Beard and asking him about behaviors, trends and lessons he observed. "Well, we have had 6 different substitute teachers in that class for the last 4 months," he explained.

"What happened with the teacher who began the year?" I asked.

"She did well for the first month or so, but things began to get difficult for her after the students got comfortable with each other. She quit in September."

I knew exactly what that meant. Once students get comfortable with each other, there is more joking around, students are more likely to talk to each other (even during class) and as a teacher, students are less likely to uphold rules you have set in place in the beginning of the school year. It is important to revisit and revise classroom principles that aren't working but most importantly, you must stay *consistent, firm and fair*. A firm and consistent teacher who is viewed as "unfair" will result in rebellion. It is seen all throughout history (American Slavery, The American Revolutionary War, The Angolan War of Independence, Civil Rights Movement, The Separate but Equal Supreme Court judgment that was later ruled against in Brown vs Board of Education, etc.). Although these are large scale examples that exaggerate the point I'm trying to make, I understood what Principal Beard meant. "Do you know if content was taught? Did she leave a list of POs she went through?" (This was before Common Core shifted education from objectives to standards).

"She did not leave on a good note. She decided she would be better off in a different school and just left. She found a job in a suburban district and accepted."

"Is that legal? I asked. "Can you just leave schools like that for a lateral position?" I knew that vernacular was an emphasized section of my contract. We are contractually bound to our position as teachers unless the education position we move to was a promotion. There were a few ways to get out of it, but lateral movement was not one.

"She used emotional distress as her reason for leaving. She got a doctor's note and used it to get out of her contract," he responded.

I appreciated his honesty. I figured, at that time, he was done hiding the reality of the students in his school to new teacher candidates. He wanted to be upfront and clear to make sure there were no secrets. Since I was not scheduled to start until January 31st (a Monday), I asked, "Would you mind if I come in a few days early to observe how the students are in class with the teacher?" He accepted the request and encouraged the thought. My reason for requesting to come in early was to learn more about the situation, climate and culture I was about to enter. Being as mentally prepared as possible enables predictability and, ultimately, comfort.

I viewed my journey in the same light as moving to another country. If I decided to relocate to Spain, I wouldn't just show up and carry on with life as if I had been living there for decades. I would do research on the economy and cost of living, study the native language, identify the best areas to live in, look up nice restaurants to dine at, etc. There will always be unknowns, but making the "unknowns" list as small as possible results in better understanding, beginning more competently and, most importantly, having more confidence. Since I began teaching mid-year, it gave me an opportunity to see the students and strategize, but that could also have been done in the beginning of the year by asking previous teachers.

And so, it was settled. I was scheduled to come in any time of the day, Friday, for as long as I wanted in order to prepare for the students by observing their in-class behaviors, interactions with the instructor, and procedures that were in place.

That Friday, I woke up ready and excited. I grabbed my outfit, starch ironed it to a crisp, then picked out my wing-tipped cognac shoes that I only wear for special occasions. I felt like it was my first day of school as a kid. I mean, a grown kid, because kids do not wear wing-tips to school. They probably don't even know what wing-tips are, nor are they interested in a cognac colored...sorry. I got side-tracked. Back to the story: I really chose a more formal outfit because of studies I have seen. They describe the characteristics of an effective classroom, and one of them points out the teacher's attire. If the instructor looks like they took the time in the morning to prepare their outfit and their appearance, then the students will view them and the class as serious.

I arrived at the school around 9:15 AM and walked into the office for a guest pass. It was protocol for visitors to check in before walking around on campus (and I was still a visitor until I started working). I walked a confident yet respectable pace through the campus with my head held high and chest out. Posture and presentation are huge indications of confidence. Nervousness is something that can come out at times, even if we don't intend it to. I wanted to make sure the vibes I gave off did not include being nervous (even if I it was something I felt). I proceeded through the campus and up to the classroom door. I took a deep breath, then entered.

CHAOS! KIDS FIGHTING, THROWING CANDY AT THE TEACHER AND DOING BACKFLIPS OFF THE TABLES UNTIL THEIR...I'm joking. I just took full advantage of the scripted build up (sorry reader). But actually, I walked in and the students stopped whatever they were doing to see who I was (typical). I found a seat in the back and sat down with my notebook and they eventually got back to what the teacher was teaching.

As I sat, I noticed the instructor going over how to solve linear equations and counted how many students were paying attention. Percentage-wise, about 30-40% of the students were actively listening. The rest were carrying on conversations of their own. Proximity-wise, the 30-40% were closest to the teacher. When you teach at the board as opposed to circulating the room, students tend to be more off-task. A teacher's presence can remind students to be engaged. I learned it in college and was seeing what a lack in proximity could do, firsthand. The next thing I knew, a young lady gets out of her seat and comes up to me to say "Hey 'Mister,' are you going to be our new teacher?"

I responded saying "1) You should always introduce yourself before asking questions and 2) This is not an appropriate time to ask. You should be paying attention up front." Looking back at the lesson being taught, the teacher was in the middle of explaining a seemingly important concept when the student approached me. I was baffled at the simple courtesy that was not being displayed. Standing up in the midst of a lecture to approach an adult in the room to satisfy a personal query should not be allowed or tolerated. The guest teacher, unsurprisingly, did nothing to correct the behavior.

After the teacher was done teaching the lesson, she handed out a worksheet for the students to work on. I decided now would be a better time to investigate why this brave student thought it to be ok for her to approach me with the question. I walked over to her and asked, "What are you all working on?"

"Another worksheet about solving linear equations."

"Oh really. Have you done this worksheet before?"

"Not this one, but we have done many like it. Every substitute teacher we get teaches us the same thing. It's like this is all they remember about math."

I looked at the group she was in and they all nodded their head in agreement. In an attempt to get them back on task, I said "Can you show me how to do this problem?" as I pointed arbitrarily at a question on her page.

I couldn't believe it. The students were not being given consequences nor being held to a behavioral standard while simultaneously not being mentally stimulated to learn. After a few more conversations with students and current staff, I found out there have been substitutes in and out of the class since the beginning of October (remember, I began at the end of January). Ms. Welsch, the English Language Arts (ELA) instructor, estimated that 5 or 6 different substitutes had passed through in that time span. Welsch also let me know that students would express their boredom in math at times in her class.

I knew I had my work cut out for me. I was up for the challenge and seeing the students' situation gave me more motivation. This was exactly what I wanted. I was prepared to make a difference in a school and community that was thirsty for it and I knew exactly where to start first: a behavior system.

A behavior system is a practice implemented by the teacher but is shared and understood by all. Why a system? Well, look around our country. There are systems EVERYWHERE: the judicial system, traffic lights, banks, etc., just to name a few. These systems were implemented to eliminate subjectivity and to establish a rule or a set of rules all can abide by.

At an intersection, you don't pull up and guess if you should keep driving through or not. If the light is red, you stop. If it is green you continue on. You do not go the speed you think is best (we hope) and in America, you look crazy if you drive on the left side of the road. These are rules our government implemented and the policemen enforce. However, the drivers on the road are also well aware of what is expected of them. That is why the first thing a policeman says when they pull you over is, "Do you know why I pulled you over?" I would absolutely hate to live in a world where the police could pull us over and give us tickets for whatever they were in the mood to give a ticket for, warranted or not.

When you deposit your money into a bank, the amount of interest you get is no secret. The cost per month is not a surprise and you know exactly where the money is coming from when you swipe your debit card. This is the same thought you must have for your classroom. When students come into class, they should know exactly what is expected of them and exactly what happens if expectations are not met.

If you leave consequences to be subjective, then it will be extremely difficult for students to behave and for you to earn their respect. What if one day, you wake up to sunshine and the birds chirping after a great 9-hour night of rest. You get ready for school and head out. On your way to school you decide to stop at your favorite coffee shop. You order your favorite latte and when you get to the counter to pay, the person in front of you courteously expensed your order. You leave out and get to school only to find that the janitor vacuumed your room with a new fabric softener scented carpet powder and left a piece of chocolate on your desk. You can't believe how well your day is going, but now it's time for class to start. In your first class,

Student A is talking and being disruptive, but you overlook it because nothing can mess up the great day you're having. You tell student A to get back to work and carry on with what you were doing. You finish out the day then head home.

But that night, a fire alarm went off at 2:00AM because of your neighbor upstairs, who decided to fall asleep while her pizza was in the oven. There is no fire, but since the alarm went off everyone had to exit the complex until the firemen deemed it safe to enter. You try and try to get back to sleep, but it doesn't happen until 4:00AM. You tried to get some decent rest, but it was abruptly interrupted by your next-door neighbor's dog that he isn't even supposed to have because it is over the weight limit for the complex. You wake up and think about how you should've saved all the money you partied with in college in order to buy a house. You then decide to get up and get ready for work. On your way to the bathroom, you hit your pinky toe on the leg of a piece of furniture that somehow appeared out of nowhere. Sharp deathly pain shoots through your body making you question how such a small piece of your body can cause that much pain. You finish getting ready and get in the car to head up to the school, but on the way, there is heavy traffic and rain. You end up getting to school only to see your principal covering your playground duty you forgot you had every Wednesday, so you take the walk of shame towards her to relieve her of your duties. You really can't imagine having a worse morning. Finally, class starts and Student B is talking and being disruptive. You have already had enough going on this morning, so you send him or her to in-school suspension or an in-school detention room.

"But wait, 'Student A' did the same thing yesterday and you didn't do anything!"

"I don't want to hear it. Take this referral and go"

This introduces an unfair, biased, uncomfortable and inconsistent aspect to your class that does not end well. If a student thinks you are picking on them, or being unfair, then the relationship aspect of teaching will slowly diminish. Building a relationship with students is extremely important because *rules without relationship lead to rebellion.* Students should enter class and know what the environment and culture will be like. Providing that sense of stability and predictability creates a safe environment that the students will thrive in.

So, I started there. My behavior system needed to be consistent, fair and gradual in its repercussions. I created it and began day one explaining to the students how class would go. My behavior system was as follows:

1) *Warning*

2) *Move to a different desk*. Sitting at your desk is a privilege. If you can't handle it, you must move.

3) *Exit the room* (until you are ready to come back in). Sometimes, students need time to reflect alone without student influences. I would have students stand outside of the classroom by the door until they were ready to re-enter.

4) *Parent Call*. It's always important to involve the parents when you can.

5) *Referral Form.* At this point, I've done all I can to help you in class. It is now time for you to move out of class and into the office

I'm not going to use this book as a platform to aggrandize the outcome of my behavior system. The logic behind having one was there but my implementation was mediocre (at best). My system had some great ideas but there were also many cons that you should avoid when making yours.

Pros:

1) Always (ALWAYS) start with a warning. You may not call it a warning, but the concept of notifying a student their behavior is unacceptable should come before a consequence 98% of the time. The 2% is for obvious consequential reasons: fighting, smoking weed in class, throwing a backpack full of rocks at the board while you're teaching, etc. (My dry humor). Come on. You're a college graduate. You should know what actions should result in immediate drastic consequences. Most of the issues you will face, no matter the population you're working with, will be talking, throwing paper, being off-task, sleeping, etc.

2) Involving the parents is extremely important when possible. You never want parent-teacher conference to be the first time a parent hears how their child is performing in class both behaviorally and academically. Involving the parent builds an extremely beneficial relationship and shows the student that you and the parent are on the same page. The National Education Association states that parent, family, and community involvement in education

correlates with higher academic performance and school improvement. Keep this in mind for your entire professional career in education

3) My first 4 steps were all related to ways for me to handle the situation in class. For my philosophy lovers, I have a conditional proof. If a student is not in class, then they miss instruction time. If they miss instruction time, then there may be concepts the student lacks in understanding. If there are concepts the student lacks in understanding, then the student may perform poorly on tests (state-mandated or in-class). If the student performs poorly on tests, then you may be labeled as an ineffective teacher (since that label is based on how students perform). Therefore, if a student is not in class, then there will be missed concepts and it may result in you being labeled as an ineffective teacher. From a philosophical standpoint, there are a few gaps this argument. One of the biggest is the predictive nature. Since there are so many unknowns, it's hard to speak definitively. But class time and instruction time must be protected. The disruptive student(s) you keep sending out of the classroom will need

to master the same standards as everyone else and will still take the same test as all the other students. Do yourself a favor and try as hard as you can to make sure they do not miss instruction. There does come a time when removing the student is necessary, especially when they are disrupting the learning of other students constantly, but use your best judgment.

Cons:

1) First and foremost, I did not check with the school and administration on policies and procedures. The school may have had detentions (lunch, after school, Saturday, etc.), intervention, mediator policies, a reflection room, partner teacher or many other things I could have utilized when coming up with my 5-step system. Also, checking with your principal is usually a good idea before implementing a new standard for the class. You would hate for him/her to observe it after you begin enforcing just to let you know he/she would prefer something else. Cross your T's and dot your I's.

2) Exit the room. Growing up in Michigan, our teacher would send us out of class all of the time

for bad behavior. "Go in the hallway and wait until I come to get you." Or, "Please step out of class and come back when you're ready to learn." This might have been effective in my high school years but there were a few things I did not take into account. One of them was location. In Michigan, there are 4 seasons and a lot of precipitation, so every school is in an enclosed building. Every classrooms door goes out into the hallway. In Phoenix, Arizona, there is only one season: HELL!!! (I'm joking, but heat is a year-round expectation and the climate barely has a precipitous nature). Since the conditions are different, many schools are built with more of an open campus feel. The door to my class actually led directly outside. Exiting the room may have worked for some students but it did not work for the youth who already had a history of trying to leave campus or cause trouble around campus. When creating a system, you want to make sure you can follow it as much and as consistently as possible. Each step should be something anyone can do.

3) Coming into a school year in the middle and enforcing my own rules made a few students put

up a wall. The best time to do this is in the beginning of the school year when students have not been conditioned yet. Beginning mid-year with this system was like trying to teach an old dog a new trick. Reflecting on my first year that summer, I decided that talking to them about how important it is to have an environment conducive to learning before introducing a behavior system would've helped tremendously. Also, allowing students to help create that system would've given them more responsibility and ownership of expectations. Even if I had the consequences I wanted, I could've coerced them into saying what I wanted them to say (insert evil teacher laugh).

4) I created a system for consequences but never implemented a system for rewards. Negative reinforcement can only go so far. There needs to be some type of balance. Lori Kay Baranek wrote a brilliant thesis at Grand Canyon University titled "The Effect of Rewards and Motivation on Student Achievement" where she highlights the importance of strategic rewards. She emphasizes that these rewards are not merely stickers or candy, but rather measurable and

mentally stimulating when possible. There is an importance in positive reinforcement and many studies show that it can lead to desired behaviors. The rewards created can be daily, weekly, monthly, quarterly and/or yearly. It's most effective when you have at least 3 of these in place to make sure students can see what they're working towards. Although there may be an end of year trip the students can earn, it may be too far away to consider when a student wants to act up in class. Make sure you have achievable goals and rewards they can see now as well as work towards in the future.

5) I neglected the power in implementing some type of self-reflection for the student. Often, the student knows right from wrong but may not think through the effects it has on all affected parties. Having consequences in place fixes the immediate issue but utilizing a think-sheet or activity for self-reflection within one of the steps of the behavior system would yield the longitudinal effects that truly help the student.

6) I did not go over what behaviors warrant a classroom violation. I assumed that students misbehaving knew they were doing so. I have a

good friend who told me "Common sense isn't common to everyone" and boy was he right. I have had students who have never been told that "shut up" is not acceptable patois when requesting the discontinuance of volume from another's mouth (Isn't it hilarious when people "over-describe"). I've had students who are allowed to curse around their parents. They see it as common more than unacceptable. This list of unacceptable behavior is also something I could've created with the students to give them more of a sense of power in the class.

7) Lastly, I created a behavior system that no other teacher was utilizing. There was no way to gage if a student was coming in after a disruptive last period or not. Since there was no school-wide implemented structure, we usually did not know about similar student issues until lunch or planning period.
"Student A was really disruptive today"

"Yeah, she was out of control in my class, too."

This student didn't deserve to have an entire period to repeat issues the last teacher dealt with. If I could do it over, I would've approached my principal and/or grade-level team about implementing a system across the board so that when Student A messes up, I can ask to see their behavior card. If their behavior card was full of misbehaviors from last period, then maybe it would be ok not to start them back at the warning level. Together we stand. Teachers being on the same page strengthens the team.

Overall, the system worked. Many would think the most difficult part was the students abiding but truthfully, *it was my own consistency*. A system without consistency allows room for loopholes and reintroduces subjectivity (one of the biggest things you are trying to avoid when creating a system). But keep in mind that 'kids will be kids.' You are not going to create perfect citizens of the classroom overnight. It will take days, weeks and months of consistency to implement a system correctly. My first-year teaching experience happened in one of the poorest districts in the nation. Many students came from broken or single-parent homes and had little-no consistency. Studies show that students in low-income areas are more likely to have a change in address and phone number. Since, on average, teachers last less than two years, then students are also more likely to have a change in instructor as well (like when I began teaching, for example). I had students on house arrest, three students who were known gang members, a few pregnant students and a plethora of other realities that students face outside of school. If I thought I was going to change these students overnight, then I chose the wrong school to teach in. It takes patience and consistency and the belief that some of the **GREATEST** minds our world will ever see are just waiting to be discovered and encouraged.

The initial introduction usually results in a few "Are you serious?" or "Oh you 'trippin'" type of responses (direct quotes from my students). But, when you explain why you're implementing, then students will definitely be more receptive. Growing up, I can recall being told by my mother to do something. If I ever worked up enough courage to ask "Why?" the response would be "Because I said so." The students we work with now are being brought up in a different era. The concept of "Do what you're told and do not ask questions" does not sit as well with our new generation of learners. Even the new standards no longer want students to merely answer a question. Many questions are "Explain why this answer makes sense." We must appeal and adapt to the current times to stay relevant and effective. If you are going to go into a 21st century classroom with a 20th century mentality, you might as well also show up to school with bell-bottom jeans listening to your favorite tunes on a cassette player. Meet the students where they are and push them to be greater. Explaining concepts and the purpose behind newly created systems will give you greater success when implementing.

The difficulty in remaining consistent fluctuates periodically. My first day or two were easy for me to stay consistent. I became 'Captain Correct-a-Student' instantly, paying attention to make sure I caught and corrected the misbehaviors students exhibited. But then, the skilled loophole-finding students got to work. I'll be the first to tell you, no matter what system you create, a student will find a soft spot in it. My students were no different. They cleverly recognized that coughing and sneezing were acts my system did not allot repercussions for. I would hear students fake coughing loud enough to get a reaction. Sometimes, I would also hear an exaggerated sneeze while I was teaching. You will always find out that the students have masterminded a strategy to safely get around following rules and you must act in one of two (or both) ways:

1) *Ignore*! Students are usually looking for a reaction. If you give none, they will recognize their attempt as a failure and the action will

slowly go away (hopefully). If it doesn't, or is an action that warrants more than simply ignoring, then...

2) *Modify your system*. As a professional, you should be constantly revisiting your craft to make progressive revisions and your classroom management should be no different. Businesses put products out all the time then have to modify it based on customer reviews and reactions. How many car recalls have you heard of? How many times did Facebook change? Think about the iPhone and all the changes it has gone through. Your classroom and craft are no different: you must be willing to change if necessary.

One thing you absolutely should not do is take the students' behavior personally. Michael Linsin had an article published on smartclassroommanagement.com with some important things to consider about taking student actions personally:

> "One of the biggest classroom management mistakes teachers make is that they take disrespectful behavior personally. To quote Tom Hagen speaking to Sonny Corleone in the classic movie *The Godfather*, "This is business, not personal." When you take disrespectful

behavior personally, two things are likely to happen:

1) You will desire to get even, to show your students who is boss;

2) you will be inclined to scold, lecture, or react with sarcasm.

Both will encourage more disrespectful behavior from your students. When you react angrily or with spite, you cause your students to resent you, resulting in more of the same unwanted behavior. I've heard teachers say that they don't care if they're disliked, that it isn't their job to have students like them. This may be true, but it will make you a less effective teacher and make classroom management more difficult. Taking poor student behavior personally sends the message to your students that they can push your buttons and disrupt your day if they choose. **This shifts control over to your students and weakens your ability to manage your classroom."**

Reaction is a natural response, but you must do all you can to hide it. Once a student finds that button, then it will be pushed more and more.

Self-Reflection

1) Knowing the clientele you are servicing is important in all aspects of business. Education is no different. Finding out more about the culture, trends, language, etc. will help you to adapt to the community. This will also give you more credibility with your students and their parents.

What can you do to research your clientele and the community you will be servicing?

2) There is no scripted way to establish classroom expectations and the absolute worst thing you can do is use a system that you are not comfortable with. We all have different styles and comfort levels so finding one that fits you is extremely important. Will you create the rules with your students? Will you create the rules and allow students to weigh in their opinions? Will you create them yourself then present them to the students without asking them to give input? Whichever style you choose, must be firm, seem fair and you must be consistent in enforcing.

*What tactics can you utilize to make sure your classroom rules are **firm, fair** and **consistent**?*

3) There are positive and negative forces all over, including in your class. Students around your most talkative student have greater odds to engage in talking. Students around your best behaved and most driven student tend to grasp on to that non-verbal leadership. It's a simple theory called emotional contagion. Where you are in the classroom can change the mood and participation of many. Instead of teaching at the board, try walking around. Stand by your most difficult student when asking questions instead of from the front of the room. Your proximity can be a very strategic tactic implemented. It can help redirect an off-task student and your mood/drive/passion can also spread.

At what times during your lesson can you implement the power of proximity?

4) You must have a behavior system in place. There needs to be a progressive disciplinary plan that is firm and fair. This system needs to be implemented and displayed for everyone to see. When someone gets pulled over by law enforcement, there is a shared understanding of the laws in place by both the person committing the infraction and the person enforcing policies. This is the reason a police officer's first question is "Do you know why I pulled you over?" Our

students need to know what is expected of them and what will happen if what is expected is not being done. Every system should start with some form of a verbal warning. Keep in mind, they're kids. They will mess up and sometimes the just need a friendly reminder.

You must follow your system without hesitation. Many teachers threaten to give a warning to a student or to move them to step two of their behavior system, but inconsistent consequences reintroduces the emotional bias our behavior system is supposed to eliminate. Using a behavior system when you feel like it puts us back at square one. If you feel like you can be consistent with the behavior system, modify it. All great companies modify and evolve their products/services when necessary. Your job as the teacher utilizing this behavior system is to be as consistent as possible. If that consistency is being compromised for any reason, go back to the drawing board and adjust where needed.

Create a 5-step behavior system utilizing things available at your school (example: if your school does not have an after-school detention program, you may want to exclude that as a consequence.

1) Verbal Warning

2)_____

3)_____

4)_____

5)_____

How will you keep track of students who receive infractions?

5) Positive reinforcement is vital and creating a classroom environment where excellence is celebrated can do wonders for your classroom management. If there is only an end of year reward, a student can perform poorly for four months then be the best student ever for four months and still receive it. Students need the end of year jackpot reward but there should also be rewards they can benefit from in the interim. I suggest having at least a weekly, quarterly and yearly goal students can work towards individually, in a group or as a class. There can be options like a school dance or carnival, 30 minutes of

free-time on Friday, a class trip to the local museum, an end of year school trip out of town, movie day, etc. Be as creative and 'outside-of-the-box' as you want. However, make sure to run these ideas by your administration to ensure their approval.

What daily, weekly, monthly, quarterly and/or yearly rewards can you put in place for students to work towards?

How will you keep track of your student's/classroom's progress towards these rewards?

Lesson 4

Strengthening Classroom Management
Ms. Welsch

Sometimes, the system just does not work for handling outbursts. Students may be looking to get that attention they are void of receiving at home in class and receiving a warning or worse can be almost medicinal. Through the rest of the year, I had multiple issues that came up for me to handle on a different scale. One of them was with a student I had named Fernando. He was a handsome and popular kid but would never do his work. Sometimes he would make crazy jokes or walk around in class (when he knew my expectation was for him to be in his seat). In a meeting with my middle school team, I asked if anyone had issues with this student and if they had any insight on why the student behaved like this in class. There are two things to note here: 1) getting to the root of a problem helps aid in solving it and 2) do not think you have to figure out strategies yourself. Using ideas others have found successful is a practice that will make your life easier. One of my colleagues, Ms. Welsch, spoke up about it:

> "Fernando used to give me so much trouble. He never did his work and was a goof off. I talked to him after class one day and realized he was intelligent. Still, I was unaware of why he acted out in class. The first thing I thought was 'he needs the attention' and I could assume it was from the lack of it at home, but when I saw his home life everything made sense. Our principal organized a neighborhood meet-and-greet where we walked around and visited our students' homes in the area. When we walked up to Fernando's house and knocked on the door, a woman answered the door. This was not his mother. She went to get Fernando's mother, but on her way, she stopped and asked another woman where his mother was. When Fernando's parent came to the door, I realized the adults in the house were very comfortably dressed, as if they lived there. Come to find out, they did. The house we were in was a three-bedroom, 1200 square foot home with three families living there. Each family had at least two

children and Fernando had 4 siblings. There were 14+ people living in this three-bedroom house. We were lucky to catch his mother because she worked 2 jobs. His father also worked two jobs, so he was not available. My heart immediately sided with Fernando as I knew his reasons for acting out in class. There was a need for attention at school that he did not always get at home. I had to let him know his methods in class were unacceptable, but I also needed to provide that missing piece. What I ended up doing was allowing Fernando to change the date and pass out papers in class. Letting him pass out papers and be the center of attention provided a few things: an appropriate way for him to get attention, a way for us to connect outside of the content and the opportunity to take him under my wing. I also started putting stickers on his work while he was on task. Eventually he would call me over to see the work he completed and If I didn't give a sticker, he would ask for one. Not sure why he loved those stickers so much, but it definitely helped with his in-class behavior. Also, to give him a deeper level of responsibility I would allow him make decisions that would affect the entire class at times. Did these methods create a perfect student? No; but it did diminish his negative participation in class a great amount."

Hearing about his story and how he lived from Ms. Welsch evolved the compassion I had. I went from being stern while trying to uphold the rules of my class to being understanding while upholding the rules of my class. I would never give up on the standards of the class I've established. *Students still need for us to keep the bar higher than they think they can reach as we coach and encourage them to get there.* Since our students aren't given a pass in society, I knew they didn't need anything handed to them. Also, since many lacked that family time and societal structure, I had to provide it in class.

Our students have lives outside of the class and many of their realities can trickle into their mood. But it's important as a teacher to have compassion, not pity. The idea to provide the attention (instead of reacting to unwanted behavior, which was clearly a cry out for attention) was simple yet genius. I ended up finding things for certain students to do (change the date on the board, erase the board, pass out papers, direct students to their desks when a new seating chart came out, collect homework, etc.) and would allow them to have that responsibility when possible.

This ended up being one of many lessons I learned from Ms. Welsch. I actually learned a lot from her and it's funny how different our visual appearances were. I knew I wouldn't have a problem relating to the students because I am a minority, grew up without many resources, listen to hip-hop, find interest in pop-culture, am an athlete, was the class-clown in school, my parents divorced while I was a child and I did not see my father as much as I wanted (during that time...my father is a wonderful man and we have an incredible relationship now, but this is still something I knew many students would be experiencing). There were many factors I could draw upon to show the students that I know, and can relate to, where they are coming from.

Ms. Welsch, on the other hand, is a slender, blonde hair, blue-eyed, Caucasian woman who grew up in the suburbs, yet could draw upon her experiences and interest in pop-culture to relate to the students just as well, or better than anyone I have ever seen. The population we worked with in Phoenix was predominantly Hispanic, and although there are obvious physical differences, the students revered her. I had a chance to visit her class a few times and even her ability to manage their behaviors in class was far beyond what I thought her appearance commanded.

I can remember thinking about how ignorant I was to think you have to look like someone or experience the same struggle to be able to relate and I thank God for putting me on a team where I could graduate from the ridiculously small-minded box I was in. Working with her that year and the next showed me so much about how compassion, consistency, encouragement and support can help you gain the respect and love of your students. Welsch would be available after school to talk and connect with students just as much as she was available for tutoring. Students need connection just as much as content and she provided it. She would go to the school's organized sporting events (whether on-campus or off) to show support. She was genuine in her approach, but it also worked very well for building that relationship with the students that is so important to help them reach even further (and believe me, the students were very appreciative).

Another lesson Welsch taught me was the power of ignoring, as I mentioned earlier in this story. Although I would love to claim it as my own, it was definitely something I give her credit for. There was an instance, I can recall, when a student had a weed pipe (a marijuana utensil utilized for enjoying the effects of THC, for anyone who has been living under a rock) in her pocket. This pipe was metal and the student did not put it securely in her pocket. It ended up falling out of her pocket while Welsch was teaching. Because of its metal makeup, the noise it made as it hit the floor caught the attention of the entire class. Naturally, when something like this happens you want students to know that this is unacceptable, and you may get off-task from your original plans to teach. However,

Welsch responded by continuing to teach her lesson (I believe she was leading the students through guided notetaking) as she walked over to the pipe, picked it up and put it in her desk. She never addressed the issue in class and simply directed the students back to what they were supposed to be doing. If she addressed the issue when it happened, the students' minds would have been centered on the situation and she could have lost the entire focus. Since she gave it little attention (at the time), and the students followed her leadership. Right before the bell went off to signal the end of class, she told the students to line up at the door and asked the student to stay after to discuss. After the class left, she had a lengthy discussion with the student about the choices she makes. Since all the other students knew she was in trouble but weren't able to see what happened, they assumed the worst and learned their lesson about what is and is not acceptable as well. This method should not be used for everything, but when you recognize something happening that could possibly derail and distract the class, you want to do what is necessary to diffuse it.

After she told me about this story, I immediately thought of ways I could utilize the strategy. The first thing that came to mind was when students crack jokes on me. I had a very good relationship with my students and loved to allow them to be themselves. My philosophy was "If you follow the rules of the class and show respect, we will have fun." We would have a blast within the realms of our lessons and I would incorporate on-task jokes all the time. One of the jokes I told happened to be about Lebron James. Once students get comfortable, they will make jokes and you have to have tough skin. It cannot get to you. A student took the opportunity to say "Mr. Campbell, you kind of look like Lebron James." If I knew of the ignore method, I would have kept going with the lesson and gave the comment little-no attention. However, I was not aware of the brilliance just yet, so I jokingly said back "Why? Because I'll dunk on you like he would?"

He responded "No, because of your hairline." Immediately all the students started laughing. I went through male pattern baldness at an early age and tried to hold on to whatever hair I had left so it was a typical joke. But since he cracked a joke on me, I had to say something back. I don't even remember my response, but I know we had been derailed 5 mins from my lesson. Every sub-objective I provided needed to be revisited to get their attention back on the content. I could have easily ignored the joke and had that same back and forth at lunch or after class. The *ignore method* was in full force thereafter.

Because of the many ups and downs of my first year teaching, I finished out the school year with an extended list of lessons I learned and wanted to implement the next year. The irony in how much I learned from working as a teacher is hilarious to me. I knew I would be going into this position to teach, but I ended up learning just as much. The important thing was to take some much-needed (and deserved) time away from everything to refresh my mind and prepare for the next year. As I mentioned before, statistics show that teachers in an urban area, or title-I school, do not last long and being burned out is one of the main contributors. We all have different thresholds of what we can handle but adhering to that threshold instead of pushing the limit can work wonders for our longevity.

Welsch and I were the only teachers returning to teach the next year and we had many ideas we wanted to carry out to push our students even further in their mastery of grade-level content. We knew that with a strong group of educators we would be able to do so much more. Our principal already had "strong candidates" applying to take over the vacant positions and assured us that our team would be great. We went into the next school year with so much hope. I just knew our team would be prepared to deliver stellar instruction...but then, I met Mr. Mantle.

Self-Reflection

1) There's an article written by Michael Linsin that gives great insight as to why delegating responsibility to difficult students may help. Michael says it "keeps them busy, feeling useful, and preoccupied with something other than misbehaving." However, he goes on to say that utilizing simple responsibilities within the class can help in the moment but giving greater responsibility with the very real possibility of failure can transform the student.

Asking a disruptive student to pass out papers, change the date on the board or collect homework will help but what serious responsibilities can you think of that would give that student a heftier load of leadership?

2) Students can see that you care for their growth and well-being, but a great strategy is to show them you care outside of the classroom. If you only display how much you care throughout the school day, then you are doing the job you are paid to do. Students do not see the long hours we take to plan lessons, grade papers and meet with faculty, but when they see us showing up to their basketball game with a "Go (insert student's name)" poster, organizing a neighborhood cleanup, finding time to support a birthday party, etc. they will

see how much you care outside of your obligations and you will begin to see your relationship shift for the better.

What events can you create or attend to cultivate a connection with your students?

3) For a student who receives less attention than they need, all attention is good attention. They create their own supplement. It's our job to help the student but not at the expense of the class. Ignoring is powerful. It lets the student know they cannot get under your skin and indirectly lets them know they will not receive the attention they seek in this fashion. This does not mean to ignore their misbehaviors. I realize the ignore method seems to contradict having a consistent behavior system, in which you are correct, but sometimes it is necessary. There's no perfect formula for when to use it and you must be careful if utilizing it dismantles the consistency of your behavior system. However, there are times and situations where it works. For me it was mostly when students made jokes, laughed about something in class or laughed louder than everyone else was laughing to gain that attention. For you, it may look completely different.

How could you use the power of ignoring within your class?

Act 2

Then, I met...
Mr. Mantle

Lesson 5

Setting Up Your Classroom for Success
New Year, Fresh Start

As the following school year approached, Welsch and I decided to go to the school to set our rooms up. It's important for your room to be conducive to student learning so I had a lot to do. First, I put up mind-stimulating images. Students will begin to look around at times of boredom. Since this generation is developing through technology, their attention span is getting smaller and smaller. Complaining about the current directive of our society is typically ineffective but evolving our own minds to remain a step ahead is powerful. It is inevitable that there will be "times of wonder" when a student may tune out what is going on and become visually inquisitive. Either provide something for them to optically engage with or allow them to stimulate themselves. I put up real life posters that say things like "Prove the statistics wrong," or "Great leaders don't start off great, but all great leaders start somewhere."

There is data that shows African-Americans and Latino-Americans are more likely to end up in jail than in a college dorm. I planned on talking about these harsh realities (day one) then following up with how my students would be capable of changing the world if they put their minds to it. I planned on telling them how collectively, they were smarter and more brilliant than I was and could overcome any obstacle if they decided. I would also hang passive motivational posters that reinforce being college-bound, on-task, successful, etc. and would start off every week telling the students they were beautiful, capable and can be successful if they wanted (I cannot iterate enough how important it is to provide hope).

The other important thing was to hang up images of people who look like them. If they are not motivated by my success, then I needed to find someone physically relatable to assist. Find pictures of local athletes who made it big, activists who came from similar backgrounds, men and women who changed the world, etc. Students can feel like the odds are against them but seeing someone with similarly stacked odds who "made it out" can work wonders for their confidence and hope.

Next, I fixated the desks for collaboration and learning. Sitting the students in rows is archaic. If you want to bore students out of their minds and make them think for themselves on everything, then put them in rows. This concept does not mimic their reality outside of class at all. If you are seeking an answer and could not find it on a search engine, would you just sit there and think all by yourself until you came up with the answer? Well, you may; but more than likely you would text or call a friend, parent, close relative, etc. Once you found the answer, you could apply the same strategy to the next time you needed the answer. This is how our classrooms should be set up. Yes, students should have time to think on their own, but they should also be encouraged to collaborate with fellow classmates (group work is usually a great strategy for students with learning disabilities as well). I planned on putting them in groups of 4. I found a great concept for assigning groups and wanted to try it out:

Write down your students in one column in order from most mathematically competent (or whatever your content is) to least competent then cut the list in half and snake order them in the second column like this:

1	8
2	7
3	6
4	5

To make your groups of 4, pair your first row from the top with the last row; second row from the top with the second row from the bottom; third from the top with the third from the bottom; etc.

Group 1: 1,8,4,5

Group 2: 2,7,3,6

This allows every group to have a strong, a struggling and two "in-between" students, ensuring that every group is diverse. Please steal this idea if you like it. I cannot give myself credit for this method but works very well.

After deciding on a setup for the desks, I began to think about how I wanted to implement the behavior system. I knew that simply telling students what level of the behavior system they were on would not be good enough. Building self-efficient students requires students to be able to remind themselves what they've already been reprimanded for. I decided that in addition to the behavior chart moving from class to class, I would also write the system on the top right of my whiteboard with space between each step for me to write students names when necessary. This would eliminate the need for me to memorize and would also allow students to know where they stand.

As I was finishing up my room, my principal walked in excited about the new science and social studies teachers he hired. "Looks like we're going to have a strong team this year. I'm pretty excited about the talent we were able to find."

"Oh really?" I responded.

"Yeah. The science teacher used to work here years ago. He left to earn his master's degree but now he's back. He was great with the students. He's from Detroit as well."

"Sweet!" I replied. "What about the Social Studies teacher?"

"He moved here from Oregon for this job. He has 10 years of experience and he was very motivated to work with inner-city youth. I'm pretty excited to have another teacher with a heart that big on the team."

I want to take a break from the story for a minute because this is the exact reason I'm writing this book.

Our teachers who make the admirable decision to work with inner-city students need to be prepared for the task at hand. The reality of an impoverished area is much different than a middle-class, progressive, urban or rural society. You are essentially entering into new territory and preparation is the key for success. The truth is that universities do a great job giving general education, but it is impossible for them to tailor an educational program to every district, school or classroom. Keep in mind that no two schools or classes are alike. The "one size fits all" mentality will do more harm than help. Even the struggles that I faced from year one and year two in the same school were vastly different.

Year one, the issues I had were mostly due to drugs and fighting. We even had students who were required to wear a tether (device administered to citizens under house arrest). Year two my issues stemmed from students having sex. I had two pregnant students for most of the year (ages 12 and 13). Their realities are COMPLETELY different in many instances, but they still need you. They need someone to look at them through their reality and remind them they can still be successful. You must be able to modify and fit the current situation. Okay, back to the story. If you haven't realized it by now, our new social studies teacher was Mr. Mantle.

"He moved here from Oregon for this job. He has 10 years of experience and he was very motivated to work with inner-city youth. I'm pretty excited to have another teacher with a heart that big on the team."

"That's great. When will he be coming in?" I asked.

"He already stopped by to check out the campus, but you should see him at the district commencement tomorrow."

I heard about this commencement ceremony but since I started teaching in January, I had never been to one. The point of it was to kick-off the school year. District leaders would talk about last year's successes and share their vision for where we were headed in the current year. I heard it was informative and exciting but only time would tell. I grew bored with setting up the room, decided to finish later and headed home for the day. The conference was set to begin at 8:00 AM so I wanted to make sure I got a good night's sleep.

The next day, I arrived at the conference ready to see what our district administration had in store for us. I expected it to begin with our superintendent addressing the crowd (because that's what I was told) but it started differently. They decided to begin with a veteran teacher of the district and a newly hired teacher addressing the crowd to get us pumped up about the year. The veteran teacher they chose was an older female who spoke about staying committed to the vision of the district. It was pretty boring, if you ask me, but then the superintendent came back on the stage to introduce the next speaker:

"Thank you. Now please welcome to the stage, a 10-year veteran who decided to move all the way from Oregon to work with our students: Mr. Mantle!"

I'll admit, this seems like something an author would fabricate to build up a climactic portion of the book, but I AM NOT making this up. If you ever figure out Ms. Welsch's real name, find her on Facebook and ask her all about it (more of my quirky humor).

Walking up to the microphone to receive the welcome was a Caucasian man who stood about 6' tall and weighed somewhere between 180-200 pounds. He had a lumberjack swagger about him with omnipresent arm hair and rolled sleeves proudly showing it off. He also had a shorter hair style and wore his goatee thick. He seemed like a real 'man's man.' As he grabbed the microphone, he thanked the superintendent for allowing him to speak then addressed the audience:

> "When they asked me to speak, the one thing that came to mind was our students. We are here for our students and that should be our focus. We are here because we care! We are here because we believe we can make a

difference and that difference starts with us. So, when you are in the teacher's lounge and you hear other teachers talking about how bad a student is, DON'T JOIN IN! Remember that student has the ability to grow into someone amazing. We are here because we care and we must remember that even in the hard times. It will all pay off in the end, but just keep in mind: we're here because we care."

I was blown away. Hearing him speak about the students gave me even more confidence about our team. As a teacher, there will always be ups and downs. Students will be well-behaved one day, then do a full 180-degree turn the next. But, hearing him say he would grind through because teaching is about the students gave me a sense of relief. I didn't even care about the rest of the conference, I was just happy to have another strong teacher on the team.

The next day, I went back to the school to finish setting up my classroom. This day, I wanted to set classroom procedures for what a typical day would look like. These were things like "When you enter the class put your backpack at the back of the room, get your notebook, binder and homework out and place them on your desk." Our students weren't provided with lockers or backpack hooks and I ran into many issues with backpacks the year before (students eating snacks, a dog being snuck in, weapons, etc.) so I wanted to get them into positive habits early. Earlier in this book, I spoke about behavior systems in the class and how effective they can be but **necessary systems in the class are not limited to behavior**. I wanted to make sure I had identifiable systems wherever applicable. This included entering the classroom, using the restroom, pencil sharpening, turning in homework assignments, retrieving missed assignments, etc.

As I finalized a few of the systems I wanted to implement, Mr. Mantle walked in. Our classrooms were separated by a wall with a door and the quickest way to get to his room was through mine, so I knew at some point we would run into each other. I introduced myself and told him how happy I was to have him on our team. We spoke about the speech he gave and how he decided to move his fiancée, 4 kids and dog across the country to work with underprivileged students. He reiterated some of the passion I heard in his speech, but I had a burning question that was never spoken about: "Have you worked with inner-city students before?"

"No. I haven't. But I'm sure that if you show them how much you love and care for them then it'll be a smooth ride for us all," Mantle replied.

After hearing his speech and realizing how excited he was to work here, I spared the teacher retention statistics and truth about simply 'showing you care' and how there needs to be more strategy than that. I also did not want to jump to conclusions because it was possible he had done more than he was iterating at the time. I ended the conversation by welcoming him to the school again and giving a serious, yet cliché, "Let me know if you ever need help with anything."

I knew he had a lot of preparation to do and my room was not yet arranged to face the students, so we both went along on our way. After speaking with him, I wanted to see how Ms. Welsch felt about him, so I went over to inquire.

"He is definitely passionate, but I don't really know. We had teachers here last year who were passionate that quit after a couple months. I just hope he is ready for tomorrow when the students come." Welsch explained.

I was not around for all the teacher shuffling that occurred before I arrived, but Ms. Welsch remembered vividly. She was taught very early that teachers are not always here to stay, so she was not as impressed as I was.

"Let's just make sure we are there to help him in the beginning," Welsch said, "at least until he gets used to the school."

It was a fair request. No matter what business you are employed by, there are usually people who tell you the ins and outs as you go. I agreed and went back to my room to finish.

The next day, I got to the school early to prepare. I knew the students were just as antsy to begin their new school year as I was. Since I built a good rapport with the 7th grade students from last year, I knew many would come into my class before school to say hi. As I got settled in my room Mr. Mantle entered to get to his area. I noticed he was dressed very relaxed, however, I did not want to make any judgments because this could also have been a strategy he chose to seem more relatable.

My personal opinion: I am your teacher first. Everything else is secondary. If we build a great relationship, it will start through the channel in which I was hired for. I always start off strict and to the book. **It's much easier to ease up as the year goes on than try to be strict after you started off relaxed.** The first day of school is your first test. Students will process who you are, what you stand for, if you care, if you are a pushover, if you are a jokester, if your reputation from your previous class is true, etc. Think of them like British ships arriving to America in 1777 wondering what this brave new land has in store for them. You need to let them know you have prepared for their arrival and that the systems you have in place will be the makeup for success. This is the perfect time to set up the shared expectations that have been pre-planned by you.

At 8:05, students were expected to be in a line outside, by the park area, for us to count and direct them to our class. My first period had 37 students (news flash, inner-city schools typically have a higher student:teacher ratio; even more reason to have structure). As I walked outside, I greeted my students and took attendance to see who was missing. I actually had everyone present, so I walked them into the classroom. Since I hadn't implemented the seating chart yet, I asked them to find a seat wherever they wanted. I stood at the front of the class while students chose where they wanted to sit. Many of the students were still slightly, seemingly, nervous. There was a deceitful calmness in the midst of the classroom that I knew I needed to preserve. I began by introducing myself.

Self-Reflection

1) Starting off the school year by seating students randomly is fine, but that chart should evolve as your knowledge of the students evolve. I had to change my seating chart many times based on things I found:

- students who worked best closest to the front of the room
- students who got off task when they sat by their best friend
- students who copied work when they sat by their most intellectual classmates
- new students who did not speak English and needed help with the language barrier, since our school was under staffed for English Language Learners (ELL)
- students who typically worked well together but were no longer best friends, just got in a fight and were coming back from suspension (happened to me more often than you think)

You may not get the groupings perfect the first, second or even tenth time, but you will learn more and more about your class in the process. Continue to experiment until you find a few charts that work for your class then cycle through them every month or so. The snake ordered grouping I spoke about earlier in this chapter is a great strategy to use but there are many different options.

What strategies will you experiment with to aid in finding seating charts that work best?

2) Your classroom should be a pillar of hope and encouragement. Decorating your room can motivate and stimulate the minds of students so we should use that to our advantage. Motivational public figures, high scoring book reports, High expectations and motivating quotes are just a few of the options you have. Our students will look around the room at times and it's not always our job to redirect them. Allowing them to develop motivation intrinsically can start with simply hanging up a poster.

How can you make your classroom visually stimulating and motivating?

3) A student's home-life, desires, age, maturity, dreams, attractions, emotions, etc. are constantly changing. Some of those changes can take place day to day and others can take place year to year. The worst thing we can do is trap them in the box in our minds based on what we heard about that student, how our

class was last year or what we know about the population we're dealing with.

In my last year of teaching, I can recall a 7th grade transfer student named Isabelle coming mid-year. Even though she only stood 5'3", this girl was TOUGH! She loved to fight and was very sneaky about it. She would always fight off-campus so that she couldn't get in trouble and even instigated a few other fights just for her own pleasure. A lot of the students were scared of her. However, she was extremely brilliant with academics. I identified her as an *influencer* (more info in Lesson 6), so I made sure to build a great rapport with her early. She didn't act out in my class, but I remember thinking "hopefully she doesn't run the next teacher out of the school."

Since I wanted to support my former students, the next year I attended the 8th grade promotion ceremony. They always choose the student council president or highest performing 8th grade student to give a speech on behalf of the student population and sure enough, it was Isabelle! I was so surprised and delighted to see her up there but also became perplexed as to how it happened. I asked one of the teachers about her and they said she made a complete 180-degree change. They didn't know what happened with her over the Summer, but she came back to school mature and ready to be a leader on campus.

Thinking back on her transformation makes me wonder, what if I told my successor to watch out for her? What if he listened to the stories from the past year and used that in his interactions with her? What if she was never given a chance for a fresh start? Often times, we hold on to things we experienced with former students and use them to box current students in. Believe it or not, many of those are done without us thinking about it. Our students deserve to have fresh starts. And as educators, we should be speaking with former teachers to see what strategies worked to help that student, instead of simply what issues to look out for.

What experiences do you need to let go of in order to allow your students to have a fresh start to make a new impression?

Lesson 6

Systems to Implement
First Period

"My name is Mr. Campbell and I will be your homeroom teacher and math instructor. I am not a mean person, but I have high expectations for you. I believe that excuses are unacceptable, and they will not be tolerated. If you fail, it will be because of laziness, not because of ability. You guys are brilliant. Some of you know it now, and others have yet to figure it out. But, that's why I am here. I'm going to work with you to push you further than you thought you could go. We are going to go there together as a team and our school year will be great. There are a few things I want to bring to you..."

"You seem really strict mister," a student interrupted me to say.

"Thank you for demonstrating rule number 1. BE RESPECTFUL. You absolutely will not talk while I or anyone else in this class is speaking. This is the minimum requirement. Arguments begin when people interrupt or try to speak over each other. We will have conversations and debates. I will respect you while you have the floor and I expect the same thing in return."

Often, students will abide by rules if they see you abide by them too. If you have a "do not eat in my class" rule but show up to class with snacks, it may lead to rebellion. Students (especially those in higher grade levels) love to hold you to the same standard you have established. If you do not abide, you will be viewed as unfair.

"Another part of our class that will be in effect immediately is the behavior system." I pointed to the system I wrote in the top right corner of the whiteboard and explained its progression. I also asked my class if they thought it was a fair thing to have in place. They responded by nodding their heads yes. I was definitely going to bring up that moment later when a student would inevitably complain about its fairness. I already had my rebuttal for complaints lined up. I knew I could calmly address complaints by saying something like, 'But when I asked you in the beginning of the year, you said it was fair.'

"Since I have a strict fairness policy and you spoke out of turn interrupting me, I am going to have to give you a warning. What's your name again?"

"Are you serious?! Aww, come on," he said.

"I don't like to repeat myself either," I responded.

"Fine…. My name is Joshua."

"Thank you for volunteering to show how I notify you of these consequences. Since Joshua has a warning, I'm going to put his name on the board under the section titled 'warning.' This lets you know that I have recognized your behavior and would like you to do what's necessary to correct it. This is just a warning, so cheer up, Josh."

Joshua raises his hand. "Yes?" I replied.

"My brother told me that you were the coolest teacher. Is that true?"

I could already sense that Josh would be one of the more vocal students. I had his brother the year before and it was true, we had a great time together. "I might be, but we have to get the rules down first. This brings me to the next part of our first day. We are going to practice how to enter the classroom. You are expected to enter quietly. I'm ok with a calm or low chatter but you may not scream. If you enter the class loudly, I will ask you to exit and we will try it again as if we were 3rd graders. As you enter the class, you will grab your notebook, pencil and bellwork sheet out of your backpack then sit at your desk. This is a weekly bellwork sheet that you must maintain," I said as I held up a copy of the template. "I collect them every Friday. If you lose yours, you can find a new one here. Since I stamp completed bellwork assignments daily, losing it will cost you a few points. As you sit, there will be a task or problem projected on the board for you to work on. You will have 7 minutes to complete whatever is written before we talk about it. Let's try this to see if we get it right. Everyone stand up, go outside and line back up."

The students got up and went outside to line up. I met them out there and pretended like this was their first time entering. "Hello. Welcome to class." I said as I shook their hands to greet them. They entered the class, placed their backpacks at the back of the room and sat down. Everyone followed the rules to the tee, but 6 or 7 forgot to grab a bellwork sheet. "Alright. Let's try it again. We need 100% to move on."

"Why? Can't you just make those students do it again?" a student said.

"We are a team. You could have helped them remember to get a bellwork sheet. Why didn't you remind them to get it out of the bin I showed you? We are so much stronger together. You need to be accountable for the class. If you see someone doing something incorrect, help them out. If you see someone off task, redirect them. Please go outside and let's try this again."

As the students walked outside, I heard a few grunts and displeased tones. I even heard someone say, "Ok, if you didn't get a bellwork sheet out of the bin, make sure you get it. They're in the back of the room on the table next to the area where we put our backpacks."

PERFECT!! My strategy was working. I wanted to establish them as a team. Peer-to-peer interactions are so vital to a student's progression. Correction doesn't always need to come from an authoritative figure. Building my class to be efficient and self-motivated would work in my favor and aid in pushing them to higher levels of achievement. We went back outside and tried again. This time they got it right.

"Great job guys. Now that you understand what I expect, let's work on our first bellwork assignment."

Projected on the board was a basic introductory type of assignment asking for their name, age, something special about them and the grade they want to get in class. Since this bellwork assignment was short, I put a timer on the display and only gave them three minutes to finish. It is always important to set mini-deadlines during class that are visible to all. Three minutes to one student might conceptually feel different than three minutes to another. I struggled with that in my first year. I would often hear things like 'it hasn't been three minutes yet.' The visible timer makes sure all are on the same page.

After the timer went off, I chose a student at random by using popsicle sticks. All of their names were written on a popsicle stick and placed into a jar. There are many apps you can download to your phone that now serve as a student randomizer. Implementing a random student selector aids in student accountability. Many times, teachers ask students to raise their hand to answer. These are two reasons why that method is absolutely terrible:

> 1) If a student did not do the assignment or question, they are let off the hook. If you do not raise your hand, you will not be called on.

> 2) If a student did not know how to do the assignment or question, they would not be compelled to figure it out. We want to build driven students, not lazy students.

"Jaime," I announced.

"It's pronounced 'Hai-may,'" a student responded.

"I'm sorry, Jaime." (I said it correctly that time), "Please choose one of the questions you answered and tell us your answer."

"A" as he answered what grade he wants.

"Thank you for sharing. I would like you, however, to speak in complete sentences. You guys are too old to give basic answers. Whenever you answer a question in class or on an assignment, you will be given full credit only if it is written in complete sentences."

I was teaching in largely Hispanic school where there were many students who were English Language Learners (ELL). Speaking in complete sentences allows for greater English discourse and was a strategy I wanted to use to help. Dr. Kathy Cooter of Bellarmine University said "there is a strong relationship between MLU* and reading- the oral language link. In classrooms where teachers demand that children and adults use the rule of 5 – I speak in complete sentences and their hand as a visual reminder, language skills jump even faster than if a speech therapist came in to do language enhancement activities."

"I want an A in math class," Jaime said.

"Great! Glad to hear that." I responded. I called on two more students to share then handed my weighted grade scale out to explain how grades would be accumulated. I also listed ways to make up missing assignments and tests and hours for tutoring before and after school. Before I knew it, class was over. It was a half day, so I only expected to see each class for 50 minutes. The bell rang and the students stood to their feet to leave.

"EXCUSE ME! Who told you that you can leave? The bell does not dismiss you, I do. Please sit back down."

More grunts and displeased tones echoed under the students' breath.

"I dismiss you by group and the group whose area is completely clean with no trash around their chairs will be first to be dismissed."

It's important to establish respect for each other, but respect for the classroom is just as necessary. This method of dismissing students would help with the cleanliness of the room and the occasional artist who decided to sneakily draw on the desk. Building up the students to be a team and to be held accountable for each other also helped with keeping the room clean. They knew that one could mess it up for them all.

It was the first day of school and the students had not made a mess, so I dismissed their tables one at a time until they all received permission to leave. As they left, I asked Joshua (the student with the outburst in the beginning of class) to stay after. After all the students left, I thanked him for assisting me in demonstrating how the behavior chart worked and made some joke about how I needed to set the tone and that he was right on cue. I also let him know that he wasn't in any sort of trouble and that I was happy to have him in my class.

I asked Joshua to stay after for two very specific reasons: 1) Rules without relationships lead to rebellion. I knew that building a relationship was very important for our progression and 2) I identified Joshua as a class influencer. Your classroom is built up of 3 types of students: leaders, followers and the indifferent.

> **Leaders** are the biggest influencers in your class. They have the most power (amongst the students) to shift the climate where they want it to go. They create the wave.

> **Followers** are the students who do not create or cause a shift often, but they will join in. They typically ride the wave created. There will be more followers than leaders. Once you identify

who the leaders are, it's important to get them on your side. Since they can have an impact on the climate of your classroom, gaining their endorsement usually leads to a greater buy in from the class.

The indifferent could care less about the wave. They will be who they are everyday no matter if everyone is on or off task. It's hard to predict how many of these will be in each class, but they are usually not hard to deal with. One of my strategies for starting the year off was to identify the influencers early and build a relationship with them.

I was very happy about how first period went. I want you as the reader to recognize the systems I had in place:

-      Entering class
-      Bellwork
-      Speaking in complete sentences
-      Behavior
-      Timer
-      Student Randomizer
-      Exiting class

Anywhere systems are not in place leaves room for the student's mind to decide what is right and wrong. This may seem like a lot, but it was not difficult. My wife will tell you that I am not the most organized person, but once you establish expectations and actually follow through consistently, it becomes as routine as clockwork.

Self-Reflection

1) Having a behavior system is important, but that same concept and theory can also be applied to other areas of your classroom. It's hard for a student to meet expectations when explicit expectations have not been explained. Remember, common sense isn't common to everybody. There are many areas where systems should be in place: pencil sharpening, using the restroom, blowing your nose, entering the class, exiting the class, making up missing assignments, etc.

Besides behavior, what other systems can you put in place as procedures for students to follow?

2) Peer-to-peer accountability can work in your favor. You students need to be able to safely critique and correct each other. Once they feel this comfort and understand we are all in this together, then correction will not have to always come from the teacher.

How can you build the comradery and student-to-student accountability within your class?

3) A timer is extremely important. How many times have we had a friend say 'I'll be there in 5 minutes' but show up much later as if he stood by his word? Time does not equate in everyone's mind in the same way. Incorporating a timer whenever there is a task to complete also introduces a sense of urgency. When students see how much time they have to finish, they spend less time off-task.

During what activities can you incorporate a timer within your day? How can you make sure the timer is visible?

4) Every student will fall into one of these categories: *influencer, follower, indifferent*. You will only have a hand full of influencers in your class and it's important to get them to buy into the class. They can either work for you or against you. Since the bulk of your students will fall in the follower category, once you get the influencers on-board, many of the others will fall in-line. Getting influencers on your side can be as easy as giving them greater responsibility in class, showing up to their sporting events, cracking jokes with them or

even calling home to say how amazing the student's day was. Whatever the method, try to identify who they are and get them on your side as soon as possible.

What methods will you use to identify the Influencers in your class? What can you do to help get them on your side?

Lesson 7

Strategies to Avoid
The Aftermath

I was excited about the next class period. I thought my first class session went very well and I was pretty confident about continuing the same method for my new students entering. I began giving them the same speech about high expectations and procedures for my class. We went through the same routines of practicing how to enter into the class and being accountable for each other. I spoke to them about behavior and how they were expected to capitalize on the time I allotted. I expressed my desire for them to be successful and how I will do all I can to assist. As I presented the grade requirements and weights, I started to hear chatter next door.

The barrier separating Mr. Mantle's room from mine was not soundproof and I could hear Mr. Mantle talking during first period. I couldn't make out what he was saying because it sounded like a man speaking from a distance, but I could hear him. What I heard during 2nd period was more than just a man's voice. I began to hear students talking. This chatter became louder and louder as the class period went on. I even began to hear things being thrown. It wasn't loud, but it was definitely attention grabbing. I tried to block it out and continue walking the students through the rubric I created, but even my students were starting to become distracted. Eventually it got to a point where I had to address what was going on.

"You will NOT act like that in this class. I will not tolerate it. You are here to learn and that will be our focus. That type of behavior is unacceptable in this class and in this school." I hate that I had to make an example out of the other class, but I wanted students to know what was and was not acceptable.

What confused me the most was how he allowed the students to get to that point. Usually, students are not rowdy on the first day because they're still trying to figure you out as a teacher. I wanted to know what was going on. After 2nd period was lunch. Once I dismissed my students, I went into Mantle's class to check on him, but he wasn't there. There was, however, balled up paper, candy wrappers and a few of his history books on the floor. Welsch's classroom was on the other side of the wall adjacent to the wall we shared (wait, that's kind of confusing. Imagine a square split into two rows and two columns. I was in the bottom left, Mantle was in the top left and Welsch was in the top right with science on the bottom right). Since I didn't see him, I continued over to Welsch's room to see if she could hear his class. She expressed the same concerns I had. The thing that caught my attention most was when she said, "Those were the same kids I had in first period and they were so well-behaved." Perplexed as to why second period went like that, we both decided we wouldn't overreact and just needed to speak with him after school.

I went back into my room to prepare for the next class and left the door open so that I could check on him when he came back (the only other exit for his class was through the lunch room so he didn't necessarily need to walk through my class to get back). Mantle returned with about eight or nine minutes left before our third period started. Apparently, he was in the office making copies because he walked in with a stack of papers. I apprehensively approached him saying, "Hey, how's everything going?"

"It's going well! My first class was awesome, but the second class talked a lot more. But hey, kids will be kids, right?"

"Oh ok. Cool. Well, let me know if you need anything," I said as I went back into my room. You know how sometimes people need to learn the hard way. I felt like this was going to be one of those moments. I didn't want to be too forward, so I left it alone.

You would think Mantle had two more opportunities to make a first impression in the 3rd and 4th period, but that wasn't quite the case. All of our students had lunch together and it can be assumed that 'Mantle's class is so easy,' 'You can do whatever you want in there' or 'We didn't listen to him and he didn't even do anything about it' type of conversations took place, because disruptive behavior was on full display the rest of the day.

The same students who were well-behaved and on-task in other classes were unruly and disrespectful in his. It's not like Mr. Mantle just sat there and did nothing. I heard him dishing out timeouts and telling students they shouldn't be cursing in class. I also heard chatter while he was explaining something to his class. Once my fourth period (the last class) ended, we had about 40 minutes for our planning. I can remember that moment like it was yesterday: I released my students and closed my door. As I walked to my desk, the door leading to Mantle's room opened and he walked in.

He had a displeased façade, walked a brisk pace towards my desk and said, "HOW THE (*emphatic and overly aggressive expletive*) DO YOU KEEP THESE KIDS QUIET?" as he slammed his notecards on a desk. As I looked into his eyes, I realized he was genuinely confused and earnestly concerned. "WHEN THEY COME INTO MY CLASS THEY WON'T STOP TALKING BUT I CAN HEAR THAT THEY'RE QUIET IN YOU AND WELSCH'S ROOM!"

I felt like he learned his lesson and was ready to seek help about it, so I asked, "What do you do when they won't stop talking?"

"I give them a timeout. I swear, I gave out so many timeouts today."

"Did they work?" I asked.

"They worked at first"

"So, what happens after you issue a timeout?" I asked.

"I tell them I'm going to give them another."

I laughed to myself because basically he handed out empty threats. The students realized that nothing would happen to them if they continued acting up in class. Empty threats will only work as long as students don't realize they are empty. ***Once they see that your requirements have no consequences, your requirements become merely suggestions***. What if every rule we had while driving was just a suggestion? Imagine a policeman saw you driving 30 mph over the speed limit and issued a ticket, but the payment was never required. There was never any court date set nor was there any follow-up of any kind. Those tickets would become insignificant and we would have chaos on the streets. It's no different in class and clearly Mr. Mantle proved this to be correct.

"You have to have consequences for the students and a timeout is not the answer. Some of these students come from rough backgrounds. They may have parents who tell them things like 'Sit down before I slap the (expletive) out of you.' You can't just dish out timeouts and expect them to be respected."

Not every inner-city student has parents who talk to them like that, but there are some. I've seen it firsthand. During my internship, my mentor teacher asked me to attend the parent/teacher conferences so that I would have a better understanding of the students' lives at home. This is also a great way to understand why some of the students are the way they are. There was a girl we had been having trouble with both academically and behaviorally in class and her mother was tough. They sat while we explained the D-grade Tanisha had and how she behaved in class. Her mother turned to her with an angry face and said "See, this is why ima beat yo' (expletive) when we get home. You think school is a (expletive) joke? Every teacher is saying the same thing. Just wait till we get home." Tanisha's mom saw A tear ran down Tanisha's face. "I don't give a (expletive) if you're crying. I'll give you something to cry about. Let's go!" She thanked us for our time then grabbed Tanisha by the arm as they walked out. If you try giving a student with aggressive physical consequences at home like that a sequence of insignificant timeouts, that student might just laugh at you.

Just to reiterate: not all students come from homes like that but there will be some, and it only takes a few to ruin the classroom climate. Researchers estimate that 10-20 percent of children are exposed to domestic violence each year. This is also 10 times more likely in an impoverished community compared to an affluent community. Gabrielle Emmanuel wrote an article titled "How Domestic Violence in One Home Affects Every Child in a Class" where she highlighted issues stemming in our inner-city communities. She states, "Kids who act out at school often come from tough home situations...Instead of asking for help, they start being disruptive...which is understood because school is where they can feel powerful since they feel powerless at home." Emmanuel also goes on to argue that "if you can catch a student in the first 10 minutes of their day and allow them to feel heard or loved and respected, it can change their entire day for the better. If not," Emmanuel writes, "that one child can change the dynamics of an entire class. When a student is acting out, often the teacher ends up giving them the attention they desire and that takes away from the attention other students may need." As a teacher, we have a responsibility to be prepared for anything that may happen in class and anyone who may enter, which is why we must consider studying the community we decide to work in.

(Back to the story). After Mr. Mantle heard what I was saying, his response was "But I'm doing that. I'm giving them consequences."

"Oh ok," I replied. "What type of consequences are you giving?"

"I tell them that if they keep acting up I'm going to go and get the principal."

Mistake number 2. Students naturally "cower" when the principal is around. There is a lot of power in the name and respect in the presence. Using the principal to resolve behavioral issues makes her/him the authority in your classroom. If your principal runs your classroom, then when the principal is not in your class it will be more difficult. Going back to our driving rules metaphor: if you see the police while you are driving, often we quickly think about whether or not we are currently doing something wrong. We look to check that we are going the speed limit, that our seat belt is fastened, etc. Sometimes I'm already going the speed limit and slow down anyways just because of a policeman's presence (Don't judge me. I'm know I'm not the only one). Once there is no longer policeman in sight, I ease up and go back to whatever speed I was going. Be the "policeman" in your own class rather than relying on your principal to fill this role.

"I tell them that if they keep acting up, I'm going to go and get the principal," Mantle said.

"And how has that been working?" I replied.

"They're quiet for a second then they go back to being disruptive."

I got to a point where I was tired of talking to him. Everything I suggested he would say 'I'm doing that' or 'I've already tried that.' The truth is that there was no program in place that helped with his transition into an urban school. I had no concrete evidence on what he was or was not doing. I couldn't sit in his class and pinpoint areas where he could use improvement and if he defended everything I suggested, then what was I to do? Keep in mind, your classroom culture will tell you everything you need to know about your success. You can't claim to be a great teacher if many of your students perform poorly on tests; you can't claim to manage your classroom successfully if the students are out of order and unruly. I did not know how to help Mr. Mantle since he could not admit where he was struggling.

Day two and three were no different. I didn't understand what was going on in his class but during my planning period, Mr. Beard came into my room to ask.

"How's everything going with Mr. Mantle?"

"I'm not sure. Why do you ask?" I didn't want to throw him under the bus, so I waited to see what Mr. Beard was trying to get at.

"Well, I heard the students were being disruptive. He asked if I could sit in his classroom to help him out, but the students seemed to be on task. Have you heard anything?"

It was expected that the students would be more focused with the principal observing them in the room. I answered his question earnestly. "Yeah, I can hear the students in his class pretty much every day. I'm not sure exactly what he's doing wrong but I believe he is underestimating how necessary classroom management, and a behavior system, is. When I spoke to him, all he was doing was dishing out timeouts."

"I had a long talk with him and I'm worried about what will happen. He seemed like it was already starting to be too much. Could you check on him periodically to see if he needs anything?" Mr. Beard asked.

I agreed to do so and Mr. Beard walked out the room. Afterwards, I went to Ms. Welsch's room and asked if she had been talking to Mantle. "Yeah, but every time I suggest something, he says he's already doing it. I really don't know how to help him."

We decided to have team meetings after school, every so often, at local restaurants to build up the strength and comradery of our team. Our thought was that hopefully we could work together to get to the root cause of why the students are acting up so badly in his class. Bouncing ideas off each other and discussing strategies for specific students could hopefully help.

As a teacher, we often feel like we have to come up with everything on our own. There's no need. Search the internet and talk with colleagues about things that work in their class. There is no need to reinvent the wheel. Add your own flare to make it fit your teaching style but learn from others. We are all in this together and it will only strengthen our abilities. We were indirectly trying to get Mr. Mantle to adopt this mentality and we thought it was beginning to work.

The next few school days were pretty similar as far as disruptions in his class. After talking to him, I was sure he had been trying a few different things, but at that point he was playing catch-up. The first day is extremely important for tone setting. Once you show the students who you are, they believe it. I really didn't know how to help him without seeing his class in action but there were 130 others who had been in his class. I decided to ask a few of them.

I had built up a pretty good relationship with many of my students and they would come into my class at lunch to talk. Students are very aware. Asking them their thoughts is usually an enlightening opportunity. I use this strategy in my class often, especially if I'm trying something new. I've asked them for their thoughts on a project I created, the behavior system and if it was working or not, and even about the school overall and what would make it better. They may not be adults (or even anywhere near, for my elementary educators) but they can give you a direct perspective that staff cannot provide. They hear things on the playground or after school that students would shield if adults were around (which is another reason building a relationship could get you very far).

(Break from story) I can recall one day, I dished out 10-13 warnings and had to switch a few students' desks. I had no clue why they were acting up so bad this day, so I just stopped my instruction and asked "Alright guys. What's going on today? You know I don't allow this type of behavior."

"Dude, there was a fight before school at the playground around the corner. That girl got beat up bad!" one student said.

"But it wasn't her fault, she kept slipping and falling," another chimed in.

"But she held her own. Everyone wanted her to lose anyways because she's always talking smack," a third student chimed in (smack means talking trash, insulting or casting doubt on a person's ability).

I had to stop them. "Thank you for being honest, but you know my policy. If you want to talk about this now, I'll just have you all come in during lunch and recess and we can work on math then. I give you this time to work. Make sure you use it. Anything else about this fight will result in one minute taken from your lunch."

After hearing about this, I notified administration. You never want to get caught up in knowing information about incidents that you do not reveal to your administration (I.E. the late Joe Paterno; Rick Pitino etc.). You can be reprimanded for information if when it is exposed, you are disclosed as someone who knew the whole time. I would've never known any of this unless I asked the students. Use that strategy when applicable.

(Back to story). The next lunch period, I asked the students what was going on in Mr. Mantle's class and why they were always so loud.

"He lets us do whatever we want. He keeps giving us timeouts, but they don't really mean anything," one student said.

"Yeah and we get bored. I don't really do anything but laugh at the other students. Other than that, I get my work done," the other student said.

"Yeah, but he lets us," the first student responded.

"What do you mean by 'he lets you'?" I asked.

"Eventually he gets tired of talking to us and he'll just let us talk while we work," he responded.

"Does he collect the work?" I asked.

"Sometimes, but not always," one of them said as the other nodded in agreement

"What happens if he collects the work and a student is not done?" I asked.

"Nothing," they simultaneously said.

"Well this is what I need from you," I responded, "You both need to be better leaders. Eventually, you will be going to high school and it is important that you learn how to be leaders soon. When the students are acting up, try to help Mr. Mantle out. He's here because he really cares about you all and it sucks that your peers are putting him through this."

They felt guilty and agreed that they would try to help. The two students I spoke with were definitely leaders in the class. I knew asking students who didn't influence the class tone would yield little results. I asked them because I thought they could make a difference. I was also well aware that Mantle needed a professional makeover. Based on their comments, he did not have consequences for misbehavior, he gave up on managing the class and had little-to-no expectations for the work if students decided not to complete it.

Self-Reflection

1) It's important to have accountability partners to help with your growth. Many times, partner teachers are putting up with similar behaviors and have tried strategies that work. Everyone has a unique background and set of experiences. Utilizing the people around you to aid in your personal growth will allow you to learn from their wisdom and apply it to teaching. Remember, we will be learners forever.

Who (at your school) can you connect with to bounce ideas off? How often do you think you should connect with them?

2) Teachers aren't the only ones you can ask when you need an opinion on what will help with the students. Another great source: the students. You would be surprised how much they're willing to disclose. I have gone to students to ask if a project I made seemed legit, to ask if the groups I made would work and even to inquire about gossip I heard and want to confirm. I heard about a fight in the bathroom once and it's typical because there are no cameras or staff present. Many times, they choose the bathroom to fight because it's highly likely no one will find out. When I heard about the fight, I asked a few students and they

told me all about it (more reason to build a great rapport).

Identify students you would love to bounce ideas off of.

3) The principal is the overseer of the school. Her/his job is to handle situations when they get out of hand or after the referral is created. She/he should not be used as a scare tactic to gain control of your classroom. You are the power in your room. Using the behavior system and classroom expectations (with consistency) will allow you to have the power. Keep those pieces intact and remain the authority in your classroom.

4) We may have the behavior system working very well in our class, but the students can still get bored. If this is the case, then it may be because your content is not relatable. I remember one lesson I taught where I looked around and students seemed to be completely disengaged. Often times you get a few who need to be pushed to work but this day it was most of the class. I decided to ask what was going on and a student said, "I don't know how many hearts there are in a deck of cards. Actually, I don't know anything about cards." We were working on probability and the questions from the workbook were referencing playing cards. The

students did not grow up playing cards and had no clue what it encompassed, which resulted in them being off-task and disengaged. It's important for us to make content relatable. Most textbook and education companies are for-profit vendors who appeal to the most demanding market. In America, that is Texas and California. You may be teaching with a book or curriculum that was never tailored for your demographic, which is where we come into play. There are many simple things we can do to make content more relatable. Here are a few:

1) *Change names.* 'John walked 5 yards' is nowhere near as interesting as 'Beyoncé walked 5 yards.' Sometimes you can even incorporate students' names from within the class.

2) *Appeal to students' interests.* Knowing what your students find interesting can help when it's time to choose an article or activity for them to do. Try giving out a student interest survey to students in the first few days of school to help you know more about what appeals to them. Since student interests change often, try using strategies to keep up with them as the year continues. Utilizing a student's interest within your content is also great for getting your most off-task students to pay attention.

3) ***Incorporate Popular Lingo when applicable.*** Language and Ebonics are forever changing, and it can help us to try to keep up with it. When you hear students saying a phrase that you may not understand, ask them what it means. If you want to make a fun content activity, title it using popular lingo you learned. Browse urbandictionary.com to see if anything sticks out to utilize for instruction. You'd be surprised how much more interesting your lesson can be with this simple change.

What strategies can you incorporate to make content more relatable?

Lesson 8

If You Fail to Prepare, You are Prepared to Fail
The Fallout

Our next team outing happened to be that day. We decided to go to our favorite spot across the street. It was owned by one of the student's parents, so we liked to eat there to support. It was about two weeks after school started and we had just gotten our first paycheck. All four of us walked over, ordered our food and sat down. That's when Mr. Mantle told us.

"I have to tell you guys something. I've been going to the doctor's office and he thinks I'm under too much stress. It's starting to become a health hazard for me."

"Oh, wow" I replied. "Is everything going to be alright?"

"Yeah. Everything will be just fine, but he strongly advised that I should look for other employment. My wife is tired of seeing me stressed and I have four kids at home I need to tend to."

As stunned as we were, we all waited for him to just say what we knew he wanted to say.

"Today was my last day. I accepted a position at a college and will begin on Monday."

I couldn't believe it. Another passionate and courageous teacher who made the amiable and brave decision to teach our inner-city students, gone. I can't say I was surprised, but I didn't expect it this early. But that's neither here nor there. What am I going to do? What are we going to do? It was hard enough for our principal to find a teacher in the summer. It would be even harder since school had already started. It was so selfish of me to only think from the adult's perspective. What about the students? We were supposed to coach them to be prepared for the world. Some of them come from households where a parent or guardian might have walked out of their life. I guess him leaving proved their perception on what reality is. Mr. Mantle was given the opportunity to change their perspectives for the better but ended up confirming it.

Even worse, the students would be stuck with a chain of substitute teachers until we could find a suitable successor. But, what about the students!? They were going to miss so much instruction and wherever they end up the next year would have required prerequisites for certain classes. Goodbye, honors classes. Goodbye, AP classes junior/senior year. Goodbye, feeling like you belong and can compete academically with anyone.

After reading this story, I hope and pray that you do not make the same mistakes Mr. Mantle made. Do your due diligence in studying and learning the population you are going to be working with. Becoming culturally competent will go so much further than just knowing content and our students need it. There are so many brilliant minds in impoverished areas waiting for you to help mold them. It is not an easy task, but it will be very rewarding. If you want to change a community, start with education. Education is the remedy to poverty and leads to evolution of the mind. Many students are waiting for you specifically, but you must be prepared for the challenges you will face.

I wrote this story for you to be encouraged. I wrote it to let you know that you can be successful no matter your race, gender, ethnicity, sex, etc. The first thing you need to realize is that you must be who the students need you to be. Typically, the successful people our inner-city students are exposed to are either drug dealers, athletes or entertainers. Give them another role model to look up to. Prove to them that the world is theirs for the taking and help to rewrite their stories with a better ending.

You can and will be successful, and because of it, the lives of our students will permanently be changed for the better.

Be the change you want to see.

Motivational Writings, Poems and More

Brave Teacher

Institutionalized with crime and lies. What really lies behind that wall that they've built up? Nothing but generational curses and cries of 'this is all you'll ever be so get used to it and shut up.'

But, the mere thought that the past is anything more than a lesson that needs to be overcome is the beginning of destruction And we all know that iron sharpens iron, but the is nothing...absolutely nothing that sharpens "nothing"

"You ain't nothing. You ain't ever gonna be nothing. So, go to school and become nothing, get that job that pays next to nothing and know that you came from nothing because I'm nothing. Your past is nothing, your present is nothing, your future is nothing and that's all you'll ever be...nothing"

These are the things some of our students hear but we expect them to stand strong on their two feet; be proud of who they are. But what are they really standing on when all they hear about is "defeat?"

At least that's what they USED to hear...

Until that brave teacher with no fear stood toe-to-toe with intent to steer the student into a direction they can revere, clearing the damage that had been created their entire scholastic career. All for the one shining moment when the student can walk across the stage and receive their diploma.

But the student is thinking: "I never thought I'd be here. I never knew my future was this bright. I've been lied to my entire life, I'm SO GLAD that brave teacher came and made it right when they told me

I'm beautiful, I'm capable, I'm smart, I'm intelligent and able to be that rose that grew from the concrete. Because of it, my morale rose, and I now see my future as being concrete.

All because of that brave teacher I now know I can be who I want to be, I can live life passionately, I can make my dreams my reality and I don't have to settle for casualty!

All because of that brave teacher, I now know the truth. A high school diploma is great but I'm going to keep going and be who I'm destined to be.

I also want others to know that their name is not engraved in the pavement in which I thought my name was engraved in.

All because of that brave teacher
I'm now ready to change the world.

Trapped

My insecurity keeps me from my purpose. It keeps me in empty pursuit of worthless belongings that perish once my time is over. I find peer glory to be better than a real story if I follow the crowd I'll learn the difference once I'm forty. But that's ok. It's what everyone else is doing. Fast money is the way to go. Why should I go to school and be in debt 50k when I can flip bricks and make that in a day? My teacher used to tell me all the time that I can be better, but she left the school mid-year. I'm used to it though. Adults walk in and out of my life all the time. I'm used to it. If I was mentally challenged and stimulated, I know I'd be different. The easy route is all I've been challenged to do. All I see in that is a job at the end working for $20 an hour. Come on, you gotta do better. After all that education, you can't prove that I belong in my own lane. Your job is not just to teach me; it's also to convince me. Convince me that I can make it. Convince me that there is hope. Convince me that I can make a better life. Most importantly, prove to me that your words hold weight. If I hear another encouraging word from an adult who will leave me I'll be ruined. Be consistent and I may even become the President of the United States. I need you. But ultimately, you'll need us. I'm trapped. Set me free.

The Importance of Passion

Creating passion in others is impossible. It's already there. EVERYONE has dreams; however, there becomes a time in life where either we chase them or decide to discontinue pursuing.

Our students are usually in a position where they are figuring out if their dreams are possible or not. It's not our job to create it, however it IS our job to make it relevant. It's our job to help mold and sustain. It's our job to polish and direct.

Many times, we are the only ones signing up for that job, so we must not take it lightly. You would be surprised how many of the "troubled" students are just students with an absence of hope. Talk to them. Figure it out. Prove to them that their dreams are attainable and help them see their individual significance in the world.

They were put here for a specific reason and task that no one else on this earth can carry out. Our students are always told there is light at the end of the tunnel, but really the light is inside.

Encourage drive, inspire hope and ignite passion.

Becoming Culturally Competent

The first step to becoming culturally competent is simply considering ideals and practices outside of our own experiences as lateral lifestyles. From there, we must learn the ins and outs of a culture and utilize that information in decisions, actions and practices.

We are all guilty of instinctively considering our own experiences as a standard. The crazy thing about this is that we are conditioned to do it as Americans as well. Look at the holidays we get off from work: Christmas, Presidents day, Independence Day, Easter etc.: mostly Christian/American holidays. Anyone who has moved to America is not expected to conform to our ideals, but they are expected to respect them. What about the converse? Are we conforming or respecting their holidays? Do our students even know when the Chinese New Year is? Are they aware of the reason some Muslim families require females to cover up, or are they confused by the tradition? It is our job to celebrate differences in our classroom and not just confine the competence to a "celebrate your nationality" day. We must do more. Incorporate different names in your curriculum. Change the question "Amy had 7 buttons and sold 3. How many buttons are left?" to "Jose/Minh/Su/etc. had 7 buttons and sold 3. How many buttons are left?" Hang ethnic humanitarian's images/quotes in your room or display flags of every nation represented by your student population. Small changes allow our students to feel a better connection to the classroom and content. Do more to help students feel included and you'll be surprised at how far they can soar.

Made in the USA
San Bernardino, CA
24 March 2019